Dynamics of Power

D1563472

Dynamics of Power: Fighting Shame and Building Self-Esteem

REVISED SECOND EDITION

GERSHEN KAUFMAN

and

LEV RAPHAEL

SCHENKMAN BOOKS, INC.
Rochester, Vermont

Copyright 1983, 1991
Schenkman Books, Inc.
P. O. Box 119
Rochester, Vermont 05767

Library of Congress Cataloging-in-Publication Data

Kaufman, Gershen.
    Dynamics of power : fighting shame and building self-esteem /
Gershen Kaufman and Lev Raphael.—Rev. ed.
        p. cm.
    Includes bibliographical references and index.
    ISBN 0-87047-050-7—ISBN 0-87047-051-5 (pbk.)
    1. Self-actualization (Psychology) 2. Control (Psychology)
3. Self-respect. 4. Shame. I. Raphael, Lev. II. Title.
BF637.S4K36 1991
158'.1—dc20   91-10486
                                                                CIP

Printed in the United States of America.

To Our Students

Camerado, this is no book,
Who touches this touches a man.

WALT WHITMAN

"So Long!"

Contents

Preface To the 1983 Edition

The experience of powerlessness is as imbedded in the human condition as the need for power. Each of us thrives on feeling we are somehow in charge of our own lives. We must feel ourselves, as we truly are, shapers of the landscape, not merely figures in the landscape, as Jacob Bronowski once described it. A sense of inner control is the felt experience of power, and having choice over matters which affect us is its wellspring. We must feel able to affect our environment, to feel consulted, to feel we have an impact, to feel heard by those with whom we are in relationship. To experience choice is to know power. A situation or life event which then wrenches that vital sense of inner control away from us renders us potentially powerless. Powerlessness is essentially rooted in living, for life's vicissitudes are always beyond our full control. For example, job layoffs, loss of health or a bodily function or the death of a dear one haunt us all as possibilities. In feeling powerless, we feel at the mercy of forces shaping our lives, withholding choice.

This book is an outgrowth of my earlier work with shame and identity, *Shame: The Power of Caring.* When I completed that book, I found myself on the threshold of examining power as a dynamic motive of human beings. *Shame* and *power* stood at diametrically opposing poles of inner experience. While there were intriguing parallels between the phenomenological experiences of shame and powerlessness, there were also essential differences, which I found myself increasingly drawn to. Shame stretches differently into the human soul than feeling helpless or powerless does. We must find a way to understand these central motivations and integrate them into a coherent image of the self as an evolving process.

I was convinced that a profound sense of shame was one of the sources of excessive power-seeking, that being an attempt to compensate for the inner deficiency of shame, as well as defend against further shame, by striving for power as a way of life. Yet power as a strategy of living held other promises. Power-seeking could be kept more malleable, less rigidly relied upon, and held within the bounds of guiding values. As one example, instead of striving for power *over* others, one might instead stop at obtaining *equal* power in relation to others. In this latter sense, power offered a most promising stance that protected the self positively against shame while enabling the self to remain open, flexible, and adaptive in living life.

These conceptions of power and its interplay with shame were clear to me when I completed *Shame: The Power of Caring.* Yet the concept of power continued to disturb me. I knew I needed to understand the dynamics of power in the human experience.

As a next step, I began to observe consciously for power motives, as well as attune myself to experiences of powerlessness, within human relationships or interactions. But I did something else as well. I began to wonder if individuals could be *taught* to live from a position of power. Increasingly, the question with which I found myself preoccupied was: Can the skills of competent living be taught to others? From this beginning evolved an educational course which had as its principal objective building a competent self.

We learn the building blocks for psychological health and effectiveness in living through translating basic psychological principles into concrete, practical tools aimed at collecting self-esteem, building inner security, maintaining equal power in human relationships, learning how to be vulnerable as well as powerful, and learning how to match expectations to the reality of various life situations. My intention here is to engage my reader directly in the ensuing exploration in order to more fully *experience* the unfolding concepts and tools. Further, it is my hope to stimulate educators to adopt a similar educational focus.

We are going to concern ourselves with the nature and origins of power, not only as a motive of central significance but also, and equally importantly, as a foundation for competent living in a complex world which has grown perplexing and alienating for many.

East Lansing, Michigan   Gershen Kaufman
30 September 1982

Acknowledgments

To the W. K. Kellogg Foundation and the Health Promotion Program at Michigan State University for providing the funding that enabled the further development of this curriculum.

To the Psychology Department at Michigan State University for sponsoring and supporting the course, "Psychological Health and Self-Esteem."

To Dinny Kell whose generous spirit and wisdom live on through this book. Many of her ideas have become translated into the tools described.

To Jill McCorvie, Marlene Miller, and Marilyn Szedla who assisted in typing the early drafts of the manuscript.

To Cathy Hargrove, our special thanks. She worked hard and patiently with us in typing the revised manuscript as well as earlier versions of particular chapters.

Introduction

This book describes a comprehensive psycho-educational curriculum for psychological health and self-esteem. We call it a curriculum because it encompasses the learning of both concepts and tools, which together create necessary skills. Just as reading, writing, and arithmetic are universally considered to be essential tools of culture and necessary to effective living, self-esteem can be viewed as a parallel tool, albeit a psychological one. But simply acknowledging the importance of self-esteem does not specify the procedures necessary to develop self-esteem. And without understanding the factors which diminish self-esteem, we lack the knowledge we need to maintain it. This program is an experiment in education because it is designed to teach people about how they directly and actively participate in their own psychological health or ill health. Its goal is to help them to understand vital psychological processes and to acquire psychological tools that together promote psychological health and self-esteem.

Central to self-esteem, and other dimensions of psychological health, is shame. Shame is the affective source of low self-esteem. It is this pivotal emotion, long ignored and misunderstood, which causes either a transitory or chronic lowering of self-regard in its various forms: self-concept, self-image, or body-image; each is but a specific aspect of general self-esteem. Shame is the most disturbing experience individuals ever have about themselves; no other emotion feels more deeply disturbing because in the moment of shame the self feels wounded from within. The disturbance produced by shame affects not only self-esteem but also the development of identity and the pursuit of intimacy. Self-esteem, identity, and intimacy are three important dimensions of psychological health which are profoundly influenced by the experience of shame, particularly when it is repetitive or prolonged.

To illuminate shame, we need to view it from a theoretical perspective that brings it sharply into focus. Silvan Tomkins's *affect theory* views human beings as motivated primarily by affect, or feeling. Affect, according to Tomkins, is the primary innate biological motivating mechanism. We experience it primarily on the face, and the feedback from our own face produces the distinctive *feel* of affect. Tomkins has identified nine innate affects (see Chapter Three), one of which is shame. Because its expression is highly contagious, all societies exercise control over affect expression, including the expression of shame itself.

By way of definition, to experience shame is to feel *seen* in a painfully diminished sense. Our eyes turn inward in the moment of shame and suddenly we are watching ourselves. This sense of *exposure* is inherent to shame even when no one else is present; the self feels exposed if only to itself. The facial signs of shame are eyes down, head down, eyes averted, or blushing. The first three represent attempts at reducing facial visibility and self-exposure, while blushing is a further consequence of the self-consciousness produced by shame. According to Tomkins, shame is innately activated by any perceived barrier to the continued expression of positive affect. Whenever our basic expectations or imagined positive scenes are thwarted, shame is innately activated. Disappointment activates shame. In the context of interpersonal relations, shame is activated by any event that breaks the interpersonal bridge linking individuals to one another. That interpersonal bridge is the emotional bond between people, and severing that bond produces shame.

Shame is a natural, normal human experience that is experienced in some form and to some degree by all people in all cultures throughout the life cycle. Some experience of shame is both necessary and healthy. Shame is central to the development of conscience, identity, and human dignity.

The affect of shame manifests in various, distinctive forms: discouragement is shame about temporary defeat; embarrassment is shame before an audience; shyness is shame in the presence of strangers; self-consciousness is shame about performance; inferiority is global shame about the self; and guilt is shame about immorality and transgression. These are not different affects but different variants of the same affect, shame, differently coassembled with perceived causes and consequences. It is the overall experience to which we attach a name, and the use of different names masks the underlying unity inherent in such widely disparate phenomena.

Encounters with shame begin as partial, temporary experiences, not global ones, and the sources of shame span the life cycle. During childhood, children are particularly susceptible to shame because they invariably attempt to match their elders in skill or accomplishment, and failure results in shame. Adolescence itself is a developmental epoch of heightened vulnerability to shame because the inevitable bodily changes now under way call inescapable attention to the self; we all become painfully aware of our presence. During adulthood, failure either in vocation or in relationships becomes a poignant source of shame; powerlessness in either sphere of life is an activator of any or all of the six negative affects identified by Tomkins (see Chapter Three), shame included. Finally, the aging process itself guarantees renewed encounters with shame during old age as the body's vitality and functioning decline.

Throughout these developmental epochs, self-esteem fluctuates along with shame, rising and falling like the tide under the moon's pull. Each of the variants of shame produces a somewhat different effect on self-esteem. As shame itself varies from a partial and temporary experience to one that is more global and chronic, the effect on self-esteem changes as well. Self-concept, self-image and body image become differentially infused with shame according to the various sources and targets of shame at different developmental periods. Self-esteem is invariably dependent on the vicissitudes of shame throughout the life cycle.

The development of identity is equally influenced by encounters with shame. The process by which this occurs involves the progressive internalization and magnification of shame through its interconnection with other affects, physiologically-based drives, interpersonally-based needs, and future scenes of purpose. These constitute four distinct motivational systems within human beings: the *affect system, drive system, interpersonal need system,* and *purpose system.* The affect system comprises the nine innate affects identified by Silvan Tomkins. The drive system comprises such physiological appetites as the hunger, thirst, sleep, warmth, oxygen, and sex drives. The interpersonal needs comprise seven relational needs which we conceive to be innate and universal. The purpose system comprises the set of imagined scenes, unique to each individual, that are envisioned in the future with deepest and enduring positive affect—each person's guiding purpose. Each of these systems is discussed at length in Chapter Three.

The central idea at the heart of internalization involves the development of specific and multiple *shame binds*. When the expression of a particular affect, drive, or need is followed by shaming, it becomes bound by shame. The two are tightly, permanently linked together. Later expressions of that shame-bound affect, drive, or need will spontaneously and indirectly trigger shame, thereby causing its further expression to be constricted, inhibited altogether, suppressed either partially or completely, or even silenced at the level of awareness. And we now experience shame for merely *feeling* that affect or need in the first place. This is how we come to experience shame about crying (distress affect) or getting angry, about sex or eating, about needing to touch someone and be held, or needing to separate from others and define ourselves as different (need for differentiation). Through the creation of various affect-shame binds, drive-shame binds, interpersonal need-shame binds, and purpose-shame binds, personality becomes partitioned into parts that are acceptable and parts that are unacceptable. This process is differential by culture and by gender.

Shame binds become stored in memory in the form of scenes, which are visual, auditory, and kinesthetic representations of actual or constructed events. These accumulating shame scenes are like nuclei of shame stored within the self. Next they become interconnected, thereby fusing with and further magnifying one another. This magnification process results in various higher-order classes of shame scenes: body shame, competence shame, relationship shame, and, finally, character shame or a shame-based identity. These shame binds reflect the developmental pathways along which shame develops and produce a distinctive profile of shame for each individual.

Intimacy also becomes affected by shame to the degree that interpersonal needs become bound by shame. The development of need-shame binds will constrict need expression and directly interfere with the pursuit of intimacy. If an individual's need for touching/holding or for identification has become bound by shame, that person will be severely limited in future intimate relations, just as the development of a sex-shame bind will inevitably disrupt later sexual relations. And the presence of affect-shame binds will inhibit the expression of these related affects, further interfering with interpersonal communication.

The translation of theory into action is the heart of the program embodied in this book. To illustrate this process, the foregoing concepts about shame will be translated into tools.

> The first tool is the *shame scene:* Identify an old shame scene from childhood, involving any variant of shame from any of the interpersonal settings. Describe the scene in writing and describe the specific affects experienced both during and following that scene. Then discuss how that shame scene continues to affect you today, either positively or negatively.

> The second tool is the *shame profile:* Identify and describe in writing two or three specific shame binds. Pick one or more affects, drives, and interpersonal needs that, for you, have become connected to shame, thereby resulting in an internalized shame bind. Also describe how you react whenever those shame-bound affects, drives or needs are either experienced or expressed.

Journal writing is an integral component of the program because it deepens conscious awareness of inner events, directly engages imagery, and gives participants something *active* to do between sessions. By translating theory into action tools, psychological principles are transformed into psychological skills.

Self-esteem, identity, and intimacy are all vulnerable to the disruptive effects of shame when shame becomes internalized and subsequently magnified, growing like an emotional cancer within the self. In order to build and maintain positive self-esteem, we must understand shame, learn to better tolerate shame without internalizing it, overcome or counteract its external sources, and reverse our internalized patterns for reproducing shame from within. In order to create a secure and integrated identity, one that is self-affirming and not shame-based, we must first make conscious and dissolve internalized shame binds, re-own all disowned parts of the self, and create a new self-affirming voice to replace our old shaming voices. In order to experience intimacy, we must free ourselves from the constricting effects of shame, gain conscious access to the full range of affects, drives, and needs, and know how to establish and maintain relationships based on equal power because only then will our relations with others be relatively free of shame. The principles and tools of this program have been specifically designed to accomplish all of these objectives.

Developing personal power and effectively counteracting shame are the pivotal foundations of the psycho-educational curriculum for psychological health and self-esteem presented in this book. When the program functions as a course, two texts are utilized: *Dynamics of Power: Fighting Shame and Building Self-Esteem* and *Shame: The Power of Caring.* The program can function in a ten to sixteen week format, with two to three weeks devoted to each of the five units of the course. These correspond to the five fundamental dimensions of psychological health: *powerlessness-affect-stress cycles, shame and self-esteem, identity development, affect management and release,* and *interpersonal competence.* The additional text on shame is incorporated into the program in order to provide an in-depth understanding of shame's impact on development and interpersonal relations. This is introduced after students read the first chapter of *Dynamics of Power,* and work with the tools, and before they continue with its remaining chapters.

Educating individuals about psychological health and self-esteem must become a societal objective, an integral part of the educational curriculum. The failure to thrive is a direct result of powerlessness and shame, which together give rise to discouragement, hopelessness, and worthlessness. Leaving their correction to chance will never succeed. What is required is a new vision of education, one embracing self-esteem along with arithmetic, psychological health along with reading. It is to our schools that we must turn, and at all ages, if we are to reach the broadest population. Individuals everywhere are struggling against powerlessness, consumed by overwhelming negative affect, drowning in shame, desperate to feel whole and worthwhile, hungering for intimacy. Only knowledge will inoculate them against psychological dysfunction. Only knowledge will free them. And that knowledge must be made universally available.

CHAPTER 1

Toward a Psychology of Competence and Health

What is most important to learn about living life is given least attention: How are we to feel an inner sense of competence as well as power in the world? How are we to find direction or meaning for ourselves? How are we to cope with life's stresses as well as its uncertainties? How can we learn to feel secure? How are satisfying human relationships possible, either with peers, parents or partners? Problems in living arise when individuals have not learned how to cope effectively with these essential developmental tasks. What we need to develop are useful skills for coping more competently with reality, inner and outer. We must learn to live consciously, with richer awareness of how we function as unique individuals, and we must learn how to live from a position of power.

We are expected to know many things about living life, which are never taught us. How to build satisfying human relationships is certainly one example. But we are never taught how to build such relationships. Is it any wonder that relationships and marriage are in such a quandary in present-day society? We know at some innermost level that we thrive on competence, yet we are never taught how to build feelings of adequacy or to remain feeling competent apart from life's uncertainties. How do we discover a sense of direction or purpose to our lives? When we were growing up, no one took us aside and taught us how to build a satisfying relationship with ourselves. There were no courses given in high school or college which taught us how to see the reality of each and every life situation clearly enough so that we could know which sources of stress were in our control and which ones were not. How to match our expectations to the reality of various life situations is another crucial survival skill in a world grown as complex as ours. How do we remain feeling secure within ourselves in an environment of accelerating uncertainty and powerlessness?

Answering these questions requires a particular and specialized knowledge, knowledge of self. That knowledge must also be made widely available, as Jacob Bronowski argues in a different context:

> "the aristocracy of intellect . . . is a belief which can only destroy the civilisation that we know. If we are anything, we must be a democracy of the intellect. We must not perish by the distance between people and government, between people and power, by which Babylon and Egypt and Rome failed. And that distance can only be conflated, can only be closed, if knowledge sits in the homes and heads of people with no ambition to control others, and not up in the isolated seats of power."[1]

That message has shaped our conviction that we, the specialists in the psychology of human behavior and educational development, must pass on to as many individuals as possible our cloistered wisdom. We must ensure that sound psychological ideas and tools are spread far and wide so that all may learn to live more wisely. It is vital to teach individuals of all ages, all walks of life, practical tools for living life more competently. That is the hope for civilization as we know it. With that belief and commitment evolved a psycho-educational program for teaching psychological skills. Developed over a period of twelve years, that program has been the laboratory for this book.

Quite deliberately, we designed the program to function as an educational course. Such an experiment has its widest application directly in our educational system itself. Ideally such a course as described herein will also stimulate others, both educators and mental health professionals, to embark on similar ventures. The program was first taught through the Evening College and Counseling Center at Michigan State University on a non-credit basis and later as a course for credit. The first attracted an older population, mainly working adults, while the second two aimed at undergraduate and graduate students, clearly a younger population. This program has now evolved into a psycho-educational curriculum for psychological health. It is offered as a credit course entitled, "Psychological Health and Self-Esteem." The principal goal of the course is developing psychological health and self-esteem. By purposely designing it to function as a course, no participant is then expected to self-disclose though some, of course, will rather naturally speak about personal issues or concerns as is appropriate. All are asked, however, to practice using the tools, to report back to the group, and also to write short reaction papers (handed in weekly) concerning their experiences with the various tools.

The concepts and tools to be presented will follow the identical sequence of the course. At every step, we have striven to integrate theory with practice. Hence, we do not merely speak about self-esteem, we learn to experience self-esteem. The translation of ideas into actions, which thereby creates tools, is the heart of the course and also the heart of this book. Ideas which remain imbedded in direct experience are a vital source of learning. Hence, in teaching we intersperse concepts and theory with practical tools. We consider the concept, discuss it, explore examples, and then as a group practice specific tools which embody it. Participants also practice using the tools for the following week. Readers will follow through this book the identical weave of concept-tool as taught in the course.

In teaching the course, we have sought to balance teacher with student, lecture with group interaction. To that end, we begin each subsequent session with a discussion of participants' experiences with the tools over the preceding week. Discussion centers around individual reactions to the tools, successes or difficulties encountered, discoveries about self, unique applications, and personal usefulness of the tool in promoting psychological health. Following the opening discussion, we present the current week's topics, embracing ideas, theory, and their varied translations into action. We utilize examples drawn from personal experience in order to enable these unfolding concepts quite literally to come alive. People in our culture rarely see how a real human being actually functions on the inside. Modeling is a key vehicle for the transmission of knowledge. Many tools which aim to translate ideas into action are also directly practiced as a group within class, providing a stimulus for deepened sharing among participants. Sessions generally end with a period devoted to further discussion and questions. The course is presently structured in a 10-week format that includes meeting twice a week for one and one-half hour sessions.

There have been occasions when ideas or examples have evolved from the participants' own experiences with the course. For example, one of the tools we will consider, several chapters hence, asks us to imagine and then converse with the inner child within us all. One particular individual repeatedly had difficulty with this tool until he thought of the idea of first looking at an old photograph of himself. This worked so well that he shared it later with the group. It has since proven useful for others who have had similar difficulty in utilizing the tool in question.

One of the observations to surface repeatedly is that individuals will frequently alter a given tool to fit themselves better. Each person places a kind of personal stamp on these tools, changes them somewhat, or else combines a given tool in novel ways with certain others. Participants have also been asked to complete a short weekly reaction paper based on their experience with the tools, a kind of structured journal. The goal here is two-fold. First, this self-report keeps the tools conscious for all participants. Secondly, we secure feedback concerning their changing experiences with the various tools, any difficulties encountered, personal usefulness, and how they are actually employing the tools in their everyday lives. Many of the illustrative examples to be described in this book have been drawn either from class discussions or from these individual reaction papers.

The principles of teaching employed represent an integration of didactic lecture, discussion, group interaction, modeling, and work in the form of practicing using tools. While much of the actual work in the course is done individually and privately, the sharing of experiences with the work is actively encouraged. In the course as well as in this book, theory is grounded in action and both are grounded in experience. Your own experience with the concepts and tools we will be exploring must be their confirmation for you.

Dynamics of Growth

Since this is a book about the dynamics of personal growth, we ought to consider the nature of the process of change itself. We cannot change something until we see it clearly enough to understand it accurately. We must see clearly and honestly how we are behaving, both within ourselves and in the outer world, in order to identify the consequences or impact of our actions. We must learn to live consciously in both inner and outer reality in order to see the *sources* of our reactions or problems in living. Accurate *observation* is essential to growth, for change is a very conscious, effortful process.

The process of change is experienced *ambivalently* because change means giving up the known, which is always more secure, while risking the unknown, which is fearful in some measure. That is the eternal choice inherent to growth or change, leaving us with opposing sets of feelings about any change in our lives. The more significant the life change confronting us, the more intense our ambivalence.

When approaching change, not only must we expect to feel ambivalent, attached to the old while struggling to embrace the new, but we must also expect to *practice*. Change never comes all at once or easily; it is sometimes an exceedingly slow process in which we ought to expect to backslide periodically. This is a time to be especially tender with ourselves, to have faith in ourselves. Courage and determination cannot be taught; each of us must discover them in ourselves. Imagine that we are planting seeds, some of which will sprout and need water and warmth, their elements of caring, to grow strong. When a wind knocks the seedlings down, we have to tenderly and firmly stand them back up.

As we explore the fundamental concepts which build competence, consider the unfolding ideas and tools as the seeds we are planting together. It will take time, patience, and practice for these seeds to sprout and take root. It is up to each of us to continue nurturing these seedlings along.

Responsibility

The essence of the concept of *responsibility* is that each of us is fully responsible for who we are and how we live our lives. We need to see ourselves as responsible for our own destiny. It is not that we have full say over all matters affecting us; many major events lie beyond our influence. Nevertheless, we are still responsible for who we are and what we are, for what we become in the course of life's unfolding.

We are responsible for our inner feelings as well as outward behavior. The actions we engage in are ours alone, whether expressed outwardly or only felt internally. If we are angry at someone, pick up a book and throw it, there is no doubt whatsoever who performed the action. Hence, we are responsible for it. If we walk up to this individual and verbally express our anger, again we are responsible for our action. The consequences are ours as well. Imagine instead that we walk up to someone and express our affection. Once more, we are responsible for that communication and its particular consequences. Further, we are equally responsible for feeling joyful over a promotion or an accomplishment and feeling disappointed, angry, or shamed over a rejection or failing, Each and every behavior or reaction of our own, whether or not it becomes visible to others, embraces a set of *actions* we initiate. Our response may be triggered by an external event, but our particular reactions to any life event remain ours alone. Here is where we tread upon the quicksand of emotion: we are just as responsible for our *unhappiness* as for our *happiness*. Learning how to *live* that belief through life's inevitable vicissitudes is the deeper challenge.

Choice

The second major concept is *choice.* If we are responsible for our feelings and behavior then we have some choice over how we react to life events. We have choice over how we behave in the world and in our human relationships, both significant and otherwise. We have a measure of choice over the inner feelings we have, for instance over how angry or shamed we actually become. We also have a greater degree of choice over the ways we actively relate to *ourselves* than we have often believed.

There is thus a vital measure of choice over our inner response to life that far too often we fail to exercise. It is we who choose, however consciously or not, whether we will feel rejected or shamed or angry or joyful for that matter. For instance, when someone criticizes our actions, we still can choose whether to believe them or not. In this way we are able to incorporate only constructive feedback.

That each of us can have choice over how we experience ourselves and face life has many shining examples. Viktor Frankl lived through the concentration camps of World War II and wrote a book about how individuals can rise above even the most inhuman circumstances. His experiences are a living example of the concept of choice at work:

"Man *can* preserve a vestige of spiritual freedom, of independence of mind, even in such terrible conditions of psychic and physical stress.

"We who lived in concentration camps can remember the men who walked through the huts comforting others, giving away their last piece of bread. They may have been few in number, but they offer sufficient proof that everything can be taken from a man but one thing: the last of the human freedoms—to choose one's attitude in any given set of circumstances, to choose one's own way. . . .

"Even though conditions such as lack of sleep, insufficient food and various mental stresses may suggest that the inmates were bound to react in certain ways, in the final analysis it becomes clear that the sort of person the prisoner became was the result of an inner decision, and not the result of camp influences alone. Fundamentally, therefore, any man can, even under such circumstances, decide what shall become of him—mentally and spiritually. He may retain his human dignity even in a concentration camp."[2]

The concept of choice is a second source of competent living. So many of us feel at the mercy of forces affecting us, the hapless plaything of a whimsical fate. Yet we are more than this, certainly, as Viktor Frankl and countless others have shown. We cannot quell the waves which life throws at us, any more than the flood waters which might surround our home, but we do have choice over how we face whatever comes our way. It is precisely how we handle what life hands us which matters most in living. Defeats, failures, and rejections will come throughout life. Death, accident, illness, or unemployment will strike either loved ones or us. By living from a position of choice we guard that final freedom Frankl spoke of, which only we ourselves can ever give away. Knowing that we are ultimately the final choosers over how we both experience ourselves and face life, makes us shapers of the landscape, not merely figures in the landscape.

MAKING CHOICES

We are continually faced with making essential choices in all spheres of life. Whenever we are faced with making a choice, there are useful principles to keep in mind. Every choice brings us certain positive returns, while at the same time costing us others. Every relationship, person, or work endeavor is a similar package. Every life activity or pursuit, from career to marriage to having children, is a choice we make gaining us only particular rewards, never all of them. Whatever the choice we make, there is always that basic trade-off.

Consider Harry, who struggled precisely with this trade-off in regard to a particular relationship. He has been reluctant to commit to the woman he is living with because it would mean giving up his freedom to have other sexual partners. Yet he has equally yearned for the deepening, the sharing and security which flow from such a committed relationship. Each of these choices exchanges specific positive returns for certain others. Harry has been attempting to have the rewards of both choices simultaneously without actually choosing either of them. This has produced guilt for him and pain for them both.

MATCHING EXPECTATIONS WITH REALITY

In addition to the trade-off inherent to all choices, there are two essentials which we must pay conscious attention to whenever making life choices. First, we must know what we are looking for or expecting from that person, relationship, career, or job. We have needs and expectations from anything we invest in, anything which matters to us. But far too often we enter relationships, careers or other pursuits blindly; we fail to make conscious for ourselves what we are looking for or expecting from our efforts. It is precisely when we are less aware of our own expectations that we are more apt to be disappointed in life.

Knowing our innermost needs and expectations from various life pursuits is certainly essential though, alone, it is far from sufficient. Equally essential is seeing the reality of the situation or person as honestly and objectively as possible so that our particular expectations *match* that reality. We must see the relationship or work setting precisely for what it is, stripping away illusions. We must learn to distinguish reality from our fantasies; then our expectations from life endeavors will be realistic. Unhappiness can be construed as a mismatch between reality and our fundamental expectations of life.

Reality never matches our fantasies. For instance, people often feel anxious, but also excited, about major geographic relocations. Far too often, individuals are not prepared for the inevitable depressive episode which follows such a shake-up of our security system. That is what making a major geographic move does: it disrupts security in some measure, at least temporarily. We are apt to harbor fantasies of our new life but reality is likely to fall short of our hopes. It is rarely exactly what we thought it would be, and even worse, for the first year is often difficult. Hence, the let-down begins and a kind of depression sets in. We fare better in such circumstances if we are prepared for the let-down and expect a natural, hard adjustment following any life move.

A related example involves purchasing a home, especially the first one. Many people experience an acute pang of depression after the initial excitement: "My God, what have we done!" Far too often, reality fails to live up to our hopes and dreams, which we may experience as a dreadful error of judgment. Reality fails to match our expectations, leaving us disappointed, because we have not been adequately taught how to *see the reality* of situations, relationships, and individuals clearly enough.

Following a significant accomplishment there is also a natural period of let-down, even a depressive episode. People who expend considerable energy on a project may suddenly find themselves depleted when it is finished. When our first book was published, we were elated for some time, after which we experienced a period of let-down. Someone we know who was recently promoted to full professor began feeling depressed because there were no further heights to climb.

Relationships remain one of the predominant arenas of life where people have not learned the tools of competent living. To begin with, we have not learned to know ourselves well enough in the sense of knowing consciously our own personal needs and expectations from our various human relationships. Neither have we learned how to see clearly the reality of particular individuals in order to achieve a wiser match between expectations and reality. Furthermore, we have entered a cultural explosion regarding the pursuit of intimacy in our society. Increasingly, relationships are being regarded and treated as temporary. The cultural call is an emphatic one to live only in the present moment and to expect intimacy as something to be experienced almost overnight, instantaneously. How realistic is it for us to expect to find a measure of honest, let alone lasting, closeness with another person when we are not prepared to give up anything of importance or to risk anything of worth?

Intimacy is neither a prize to be won nor a quickly growing fruit. Real relationships take building and nurturing slowly over time before a sense of certainty about that relationship takes root. Intimacy and caring evolve within a real and secure relationship. It may take anywhere from six months to a year for a relationship to become solid and certain for both participants. Real caring does not flourish easily or quickly, but must be actively worked for by both individuals in a relationship.

The foregoing illustrations reflect expectations which are unrealistic as well as those which are more in keeping with the reality of the choice concerned. The greater the match between expectations and reality, the more likely we are to experience satisfaction in living, and ultimately, genuine happiness from our choices. Learning to strike such a match is a skill which enables us to navigate life competently. Matching expectations with reality in the pursuit of choice is another foundation of competent living.

Choice and Commitment

The unfolding pattern of choices which we make in the course of life represents essential turning points in the evolution of the self inside of us. We become known through our actions, and by our choices we both know and define our inner self.

In choosing, we commit ourselves to one particular future and simultaneously let go of other possible futures. Choice and commitment, whether to a vocation or relationship, are inner *actions* imbedded in the deeper vision of nature's human experiment. The experience of commitment is a unique psychological event which transforms the existing emotional context.

Commitment is a promise for tomorrow through which we define who we are, who we will be. To make such a commitment in a relationship is to willingly obligate or bind oneself to another *for the future*. In committing to a particular relationship we pledge ourselves to it. Commitment to one's vocation likewise involves pledging oneself to one's chosen work for the future. It is equally an expression of self-definition experienced in action.

To choose from among the many directions available to us one particular path in living, whether expressed through relationship to work or another human, is to choose from among life's infinite possibilities one future alone. Saying goodbye to other possible futures—even temporarily—is a difficult challenge confronting the human spirit. To commit ourselves to one choice inevitably is to lose another. Yet in doing so we give up the possibilities of what could be and choose what will be.[3] In the loneliness of choice we commit ourselves and in so doing define who we are, who we will be. Creative self-definition is inherent to choice.

There can be no fulfillment of purpose or definition of self without choice. To be human is to grapple inexorably with the either/or of choice described by Kierkegaard. To choose ultimately means to commit to a vocation, to a relationship, to a way of life, or to a particular path in living—to commit oneself. Through commitment we renounce the possibilities of who we could be and choose who we will be.

Living Consciously

To conceive of ourselves as shapers of the landscape implies retaining freedom of choice in a final sense. To the degree that we actively take responsibility for our selves and our very lives, we live from a position of choice. Insofar as choice becomes imbedded in our attitude toward all those unforeseen exigencies which suddenly loom before us, we retain a measure of inner freedom as well as dignity in the face of happenstance.

Living from a position of choice both requires and implies something else: *living consciously*. This means being fully conscious in the present moment and is accomplished through learning to keep a part of the self back as a friendly observer. Through living consciously within ourselves and in the outer world we are in the best position to foster competence.

Seeing the reality of a situation and knowing our available choices are two outgrowths of a conscious attitude toward life. There are a number of key dimensions to living consciously which we will explore in greater depth later. Here, we would like to sketch in the more salient dimensions. Since we live in two worlds, the outer world of people and things and the inner world of the self, we must learn how to live consciously in each domain. The inner world embraces our feelings, needs, and purposes. We make our feelings and needs conscious by learning to consult them. We are not born with a faculty for living consciously. We must work to build a conscious self, a self able to observe accurately inner events such as feelings or needs as well as such outer events as the reality of people or situations confronting us. We need to be able to see people and situations as objectively and consciously as humanly possible in order to know our choices for coping and also to see the impact or consequences of our behavior.

Developing a conscious self also reinforces our capacity for choice. Insofar as we become conscious of our feelings quickly enough, we are in a better position to exercise a measure of choice over them. If we are aware of the earliest signs of anger or shame, we can consciously mediate just how angry or shamed we become. Likewise, if we are conscious of our interpersonal needs at any point in time we are in a better position to satisfy them.

In essence, living consciously allows us to mediate our reactions. We become less automatically reactive and more directly active and, ultimately, more in charge of ourselves.

In this culture we are neither encouraged nor taught to live consciously. We either learn to see ourselves through the images presented to us in the media or we remain caught in the net of reflected appraisals of other people whom we need or admire.

To become conscious, and to live consciously, is truly to become a separate self, to live wholly guided from within. That singular accomplishment requires a language of the self which keeps close to actual inner experience.

Why have we tied *living consciously* to *language?* Because it is through language that we make known, first to ourselves, our own experiences. Impulses, feelings, and needs must be fit to words which make the experiencing self more fully aware of what was at first a dimly felt inner state. Without language, and a thinking language, we would lack the essential tools for building a conscious self. If a particular inner state, say, the feeling of anger, is consistently mislabeled as something else, there would be little conscious awareness of that affect or feeling. For instance, if a girl is told she is tired whenever she expresses anger, she will learn the wrong name for that feeling.

Language provides us with the tools for knowing about, understanding and finally mastering the many facets of inner experience. We need a coherent image of the self as an evolving process in order to create an accurate language of the self.

Power

What is *power?* To many of us power certainly means experiencing a measure of "control" or "influence." Being in a position to control a situation or decide its outcome confers power.

There are countless examples of power which is inherent to one's position or role. Consider the situation of an employee working in a business. His employer has very real power over him; he could hire or fire him as well as grant or withhold either a promotion or raise. That is power. Next consider parents and children. Parents have very real power over their children's lives through granting freedoms, taking away privileges, and exercising final say over many matters. And for the first six years, their power is absolute, for they can pick up and move children who do not comply. Again, that is power. It is neither good nor bad: power just *is.* Finally, teachers also have real power over their students, the power of a grade.

Work, school, and family are three crucial settings we all experience as we develop in which power is either explicit or inevitable. Every social group bears witness to the emergence of power through jockeying for positions of influence or control within the group. Jockeying for position is the means by which dominance hierarchies begin to emerge within varied groups of humans coming together whatever the reasons. Power is one motive propelling such social developments. It is a wellspring for many interpersonal phenomena, not all of which are destructive.

Power which is rooted in a position of authority is its more obvious manifestation, but power stretches further into the human experience than we have understood. Let us take a closer look at the nature of power. At another level of manifestation, power becomes an inevitable undercurrent, if not entirely explicit, within each human relationship. Every relationship between individuals, whether adult or child, is a *power relationship.* This idea is pivotal to the view of power unfolding here. To carry it a step further, consider the situation when we care what others think of us. Whenever we care about another's opinion of us, we give that person a measure of power to affect how we feel about ourselves. If someone's judgment counts with us, we are in a position of less power; we are likely to behave in ways to keep that judgment favorable.

In life we continually encounter individuals whom we begin to value and esteem highly, even admire. We search for heroes to look up to, for teachers to guide us, for mentors to serve as necessary models. When we have found such people to admire, we more willingly surrender to their influence, and we inevitably surrender power in so doing.

Whenever we permit ourselves the vulnerability of needing something emotionally from another individual, we inevitably give that special person a measure of power. That person may be a parent, friend, mentor, or spouse and our need may be for support, nurturing, or valuing, perhaps in response to a disappointment. To need or become vulnerable is to relinquish power.

In all three of these situations, power has been either freely given or relinquished inadvertently. The power given is no less real than power acquired directly through one's role or position. Either can be respected or abused.

We have now enlarged the focus of power beyond its more contemporary meaning: the context of *excess* or *abuse*. Power strivings have been visible as long as humans have been alive. We have also had a glimpse of a subtle link between power and vulnerability. We will return to that connection as we continue to explore the nature of power as a motivating force.

How are we to understand the power motive? In naming it a motive we are conferring motivational properties to it. Is the power motive a drive in the way that hunger or sexuality are physiologically based drives? This is not the case. To conceive of power as a physiological drive in the way sleep is required, or warmth is needed, or hunger manifests, or sexuality is experienced, runs counter to inner experience. It is the *phenomenological experience of the self* which must remain the test of our ideas. We do not experience power physiologically but in a different domain. Yet it is no less vital, no less tied to the progress of the self in living.

Neither is power an affect (feeling) in the way that anger, distress, fear, shame, or joy are innate affects. The group of primary affects comprises one of our main systems of motivation much as the group of physiological drives comprises a second and entirely different motivational system. Drives are rooted physiologically. Affects certainly have important physiological correlates, yet remain altogether distinct from the drive system as Dr. Silvan Tomkins has demonstrated. A third motivational system comprises the set of interpersonally based needs. Individuals experience at least four distinct motivational systems: the drive system, affect system, need system, and purpose system. At this point in our inquiry into the origins of power, it makes sense to speak of a *need for power*.

The roots of power are imbedded in the human infant's condition of helplessness experienced at birth and for some time thereafter. We are all born utterly powerless, entirely dependent upon the good will and loving care of human caretakers. Months must pass before an infant can reach for a seen and desired object. Watch the powerless rage which infants display in response to their state of helplessness. That is the wellspring of the need for power. The state of powerlessness into which we are born, a condition which must be endured over an extended time frame, conditions our emergent need for power as human development unfolds.

As each bodily function matures, our infant exercises it over and over precisely in order to gain control over it. And what pleasure is unmasked in each accomplishment. Controlling the hand to reach for an object that has fallen, then grasping it and finally bringing it close is to experience a measure of power. Each bodily function which comes under conscious control, from walking to language to bowel and bladder control, extends the experience of power and gradually diminishes the condition of powerlessness.

Powerlessness is the experiential ground from which emerges the earliest sense of self. It is powerlessness which gives birth to our need for power: to control our hands, to make our legs move as we will, to control our bodies and all their functions, to speak our thoughts and have them listened to, to go where we will, to chart our own path according to our inner promptings, to control our own lives and destinies as best we can. It is the profound condition of help-lessness in infancy, lasting over many months, which shapes our destiny to become in turn shapers of the social landscape in which we flourish.

Powerlessness which is rooted in our biological helplessness re-cedes through maturation. There is a second dimension to powerlessness which is quite another matter. Children can be given none or too little power over matters affecting them. Or else they are granted far too much power too early in life. How is power given to another individual? Through offering a *choice*. We have come full circle in unfolding the foundations of competence. When we are given a choice we immediately feel a measure of power, even if it is only "Do you want the good-tasting medicine first or the bad-tasting medicine?" Having the one choice that is possible in a situation enables the self to feel a measure of control which then offsets feelings of helplessness. Having a choice in a powerless situation is one vital route to restoring power. To see choices in a situation in which we feel powerless is a cornerstone in the foundation of competence.

The feeling of powerlessness as adults can be devastating, particularly when experienced in one of our primary security areas. These are: one's spouse, mate, or partner in living; a parent; one's job/career or major life role; one's body and health; and the actual home in which we live. Either rage, subdued but present hostility, clinging behavior, depression, or hopelessness are prominent feeling states which can be activated by a perception of powerlessness.

Perception here is critical to experiencing ourselves as powerless. A sudden, unexpected sense of uncertainty externally imposed, coupled with no control, creates the experience of powerlessness. When we feel powerless, we feel there is nothing we can do; something vital is being wrenched from us and we are powerless to stop it. Powerless is helpless is impotent. There is nothing we can do to alter or affect what happens when a loved one dies, our home is threatened by flood, or the necessity of layoffs suddenly looms in our place of employment. What is taken from us in each of these life-events is a sense of control, of mastery, of power over our own lives: we are rendered powerless. Hence, we are psychologically motivated by a need for power in our lives, a need to feel a measure of personal control. In this manner we come to feel fundamentally in charge of our own lives.

Regarding threats to our body, one of our basic security areas, consider the following incident. Several years ago, one of us quite unexpectedly discovered a congenital back defect which had only then surfaced and would require a radical readjustment in life style. There were many activities which he could no longer engage in, like lifting, pushing, and shoveling. He was limited and felt intensely angry about it. Though he was not fully conscious of it until much later, he felt hostile toward the whole world, for he was to be an invalid, or so it first seemed, at the age of thirty-six. His limitation would so anger him that he went ahead and did what he was not supposed to do, and then he paid the price of further pain. He felt powerless in response to his unexpected limitation and his rage was, in turn, a response to his powerlessness. Anything which seriously affects our bodies threatens our security and potentially renders us powerless.

Regaining a sense of power over the limitation came about through a number of means. Consciously listening to his body was one; he learned to live consciously in his body in order to know which activities caused pain. Fully accepting the limitation was yet another. It is essential that we accept our human limitations without feeling lesser or deficient for having them. An exercise and swimming program became a part of his regular routine and began to strengthen the muscles. Finally, learning what activities he could do, which ones he could not, and discovering some new ways of doing others gradually returned him to a sense of inner control over his own life.

Is it clearer now why we returned to the beginnings of our long childhood for a glimpse of the primary helplessness of infancy? Later experiences of powerlessness, particularly extended ones in areas of life which matter deeply to us, are psychologically regressive and, hence, return us experientially to that state. We must understand not only the nature of power but the impact which powerlessness itself can produce if we are to live from a position of power in our lives.

ATTAINING EQUAL POWER

One of the foundations of competence is learning how to develop and then maintain *equal power* in relation to others. Let us examine this through examples. The first concerns a situation involving two boys, Eric and John. The boys would play well until Eric did not want to do something his friend desired. John would then threaten to go home unless Eric agreed. Threatening to leave is a power move which can render the other powerless, and that was what happened. Eric would dissolve in tears and give in, never realizing that this reinforced the pattern. His father talked with him about power and offered him another choice for dealing with John: to respond to the threat with a smile and "See you later." That would enable him to take back his power.

Threatening to leave when one does not get one's own way is humorous among playing children, but it is no laughing matter when married adults behave similarly. In many marital relationships, one partner may in the midst of anger threaten to walk out or find a better mate. Our most primitive human fear is that of being abandoned and the threat to leave in a significant relationship will trigger that fear as nothing else can. When the threat is issued repeatedly, what recourse has the other party but to behave similarly? And so we have an escalating pattern of threatening abandonment which, in turn, stimulates helplessness, countered by an opposing threat. For some couples, such a pattern continues to the point of imminent divorce: "We've said it so often we've finally begun to believe it and we're preparing for the worst." For many, the only defense against the threat to leave is adopting the identical stance. And so we have adults behaving as little children, except the weapons are more dangerous and the stakes considerably higher.

Consider another situation. One of our culture's social conventions is respecting one another's privacy and keeping alert for the cues which tell us whether we are intruding. Not all individuals are sufficiently sensitized as we shall see. There is a second half to the convention, namely, that we ought to be well-mannered and courteous to others, especially to guests in our home. Far too often we permit others to take advantage of us out of fear of appearing ill-mannered or selfish. The following situation actually happened. At the time Roger talked to us about it, it already had been going on for some time. He lived in an apartment and his downstairs neighbor would come up, knock on the door, and ask if he was busy. If Roger had guests over for dinner and replied, "Well, we're just sitting down to dinner . . .," the neighbor would answer, "That's okay, I'll just sit down and wait till you're finished." Ignoring Roger's cues, he walked in, leaving Roger feeling at a loss as to what to do.

This pattern continued. No matter what Roger said, or how direct he was, the neighbor continued to walk in and make himself quite at home. When he asked for a drink, and Roger offered something from the refrigerator, the neighbor proceeded to help himself to Roger's best scotch. Roger felt helpless to do anything because he did not want to make a scene when other people were present.

At the time Roger laid it out to us, he was feeling enraged at this neighbor whom he had originally liked. Roger first needed to realize that he was feeling enraged because he was feeling powerless. Roger had several choices for taking back his power. He could try to accept the package of that particular human for what he was and let the behavior go on without it bothering him; that was intolerable. Roger could also remove him bodily from the room even if it created a scene; that was distasteful. Finally, Roger could block the door with his body and not let the neighbor in the next time. Apparently, it would have to be that direct and blunt since all the verbal messages were of no avail. Roger thought for a moment and then said: "But I can't do that—I'd feel too guilty!" Our response was: "You have a choice between feeling guilty or feeling powerless and enraged." Roger decided he would rather feel guilty about asserting his rights.

Roger was eventually able to "teach" his neighbor through action, much as one does with a young child, how to have a relationship with him. Once he asserted his rightful half of the power, Roger no longer felt powerless or angry. Some of his earlier more positive feelings toward the man even returned and their friendship became more satisfying. His situation illustrates in exaggerated form what happens when we give away our power and in so doing reap a harvest of discontent derived from impotent rage.

Consider a man and a woman who were attempting to have a romantic relationship though their expectations were mismatched. Carol preferred a committed relationship and expected that experiences of closeness or intimacy would be followed somewhat predictably by further closeness. Chip, on the other hand, was less committed than she and also less predictable or consistent; for him intimacy was usually followed by an extended period of distance. When Carol did hear from Chip again, usually it was because he needed help, a home-cooked meal, or emotional support. However, should she turn to him out of need, Chip was usually too busy or managed not to come through. This pattern left Carol feeling used as well as powerless.

Carol needed to realize their shared intimate moments would characteristically be followed by his absence; she would hear nothing from him for weeks at a stretch. She further learned to see that pattern as part of the particular package he was. Since we can never change another person (they must do so for themselves), the way for Carol to take back the power, in this situation, was to change her expectations regarding intimacy to match the reality of Chip. Carol had to learn not to expect that any experience of intimacy necessarily would mean anything about the future. She could certainly enjoy what they shared at any point in time, but then had to defend against expecting anything further. This enabled Carol to regain a position of equal power in their relationship.

POWERLESSNESS—AFFECT—STRESS CYCLES

Any life event that thwarts our ability to predict and control renders us initially powerless. Powerlessness itself is an activator of any of the six negative affects that Silvan Tomkins has identified (see Chapter Three). Since all societies teach the suppression of affect, this results in the backing-up of affect both physiologically and psychologically, according to Tomkins. Endocrine changes are a further consequence of backed-up affect. What we ambiguously label as "stress" is actually backed-up affect and its resulting endocrine changes.

Living from a position of power must be learned. Maintaining equal power in relation to other humans whenever possible embraces a set of skills which must be actively worked for. Furthermore, to navigate situations which in fact render us powerless, first we must keep alert for the signals which inform us that we are feeling powerless. An intense rage is a frequent indicator of powerlessness, for it is typically triggered either directly by powerlessness or else by experiences of shame-humiliation. Once we are aware of our helplessness we can name it consciously to ourselves: "I am feeling powerless," or "I am so damn enraged over feeling helpless." The next step is to consciously observe the situation to see where and how we can take back the power.

Let us proceed by way of example. Anyone who has been unemployed for any length of time knows what a powerless position that can be. We cannot *make* anyone give us a job, however deserving or competent we are. Erosion of self-esteem too often follows in the wake of extended unemployment, an impotence-maker of deepest consequence which strikes one of our principal security areas. We begin to internalize each subsequent disappointment, experiencing them as personal rejections or failings. It is then that our good feelings about ourselves, our sense of worth and adequacy, unfortunately are called into question—*by ourselves.*

Some years back we were both looking for a publisher. What we did not realize until after the first rejection was how powerless we felt; we could not *make* anyone publish the book. The first rejection certainly hurt and even triggered doubt about our work. By the second or third rejection we realized we needed to cope differently with the venture at hand.

The first step was consciously acknowledging that we were powerless, there was nothing we could do to make anyone publish our books. However, we had the power to change how we inwardly reacted to the situation. We had full control over our inner stance, our attitude, and over how we experienced ourselves.

The next step involved setting more realistic expectations. We would joke about how we were playing ping-pong except months could elapse between the "ping" and the "pong." We further decided that it was likely to take years before a publisher would be found who wanted to publish our books the way we wrote them. We could not invest in how long it took.

Neither could we invest in whatever happened to the books on each occasion that we sent them out for review. It is most natural to *identify* with our valued products or creations. Our books were a vital part of us; sending them out into the world felt like sending a part of us out for evaluation as well. That connection is dangerous, potentially devastating. We consciously worked to separate how we felt about ourselves and the books from whatever happened to them out there where we indeed had no control. After several rejections, we were able to no longer feel rejected in response. We learned not to *internalize,* not to automatically take inside and believe the evaluations, criticisms, or rejections of others.

It took considerable conscious effort over time to learn to separate our sense of inner worth or adequacy from life's uncertainties regarding, in this case, our books. We learned to continue valuing ourselves and our work whether or not anyone else ever did. That is a challenge we all face in our culture. We eventually accomplished it by detaching ourselves from how the books fared on any given venture, by not feeling quite so identified with it as it left our hands. We took back the power.

A student of ours described an analogous process which she went through. She was an artist and had learned to separate herself from her own work, much as we described, before she was able to submit it for review or sale.

We have full choice over how we feel inside and over how we face life. We have full power to determine how we feel about ourselves. Living these ideas is the challenge which life hands us all.

Foundations of Competence

We have explored four pivotal concepts which together embrace both a philosophy of living and a psychology of competence and health. These central ideas are also strategies for action.

The very possibility of personality growth or behavioral change itself hinges upon holding such beliefs as the following: we are responsible for our own lives and happiness; we have choice over how we experience ourselves or face life; we have the power to change how we react inside. If we do not hold these principles dear and live them, there is no change.

These concepts lie at the heart of personal growth and are the foundations of competent living. The more consciously we live, the better we can see whatever reality confronts us and thereby identify our varied choices. Having choice confers a measure of power; the more choice we have, the more power we feel in that situation. Living consciously fosters choice and choice fosters power. Each of these concepts is a translation of responsibility into living action.

Competence evolves through living consciously, seeing and making choices, and developing a sense of power.

The Concepts at Work

Let us translate the foregoing principles into actions. Imagine you are on your long-awaited vacation into the mountains. Over the course of that experience there are certainly many pleasurable moments. There are some misfortunes as well: the car breaks down, requiring repairs and necessitating a delay; it rains for a solid week, causing roads to be washed out; and when at long last you have arrived at your destination there is no record of your reservation or deposit. Now, when you return home with your experiences of the vacation, which feelings do you bring back and keep with you, the good ones or the bad ones?

Some people store the good feelings inside and let go of the bad ones while others do just the opposite. Consider a second situation. When you leave your office, job, or place of employment at the end of the day, which feelings do you store inside and bring home with you:

the small successes, accomplishments and good feelings or the hassles, headaches, worries and mishaps? What is the point? We make a basic choice, whether or not we are aware of it, about which feelings we store inside of ourselves and which ones we let slip away. We participate directly in this process.

Here is a tool which will translate this principle. Stop for a moment and write down five things that have happened today which you feel good about. Call it a *Happiness List*. Each of us ought to be able to find five things in every day to feel good about. Do not look for happiness with a "capital H," but the small things in every day which we usually fail to notice and appreciate: the sun shining, a good meal, walking in a park, seeing flowers or trees in bloom, a phone call from a friend, an unexpected compliment. These are moments to be treasured, and make some days worthwhile. There are, of course, days when we must *work* to find five good things. But if we can take from life experiences, however unpleasant or disappointing, something useful and positive, we regain inner power. Collecting and storing happiness or good feelings along with letting go of bad feelings are essential tools for developing psychological health.

Through consciously appreciating the happy moments of each day, we teach ourselves to collect those feelings inside. In so doing, we also teach ourselves to look for things which will actively create happiness and self-esteem.

Adults as well as children can learn how to find and collect good feelings. We have taught our own children to do this by "counting goodies" for their "goodie basket" each night before going to sleep. Learning any new behavior, and collecting happiness is no exception, requires consistent practice over time in order to become internalized, second-nature to the self. That is the reality of change: it is a slow, effortful process. Change also comes piecemeal; hence, it is more useful to look for small gains along the way. One woman who was prone to depressive cycles made such a list daily over a period of months and began to discover she had internalized it to the point where she was now conscious of the tool many times during the day. It had become a natural part of her and assisted her in reversing those depressive episodes.

When we are able to consciously focus on good feelings and events, we can restore perspective at times when depression hits. Collecting and storing good feelings is one tool for coping more effectively with depressive periods. It restores perspective by shifting the focus of attention.

A woman in one of our courses, Diane, voiced the following reaction to this tool: "I'm not naturally an optimistic person and I need these lists to remind myself there are some good things that happen every day. I'm finding that I'm more aware of the things which arouse happy feelings within me and I'm becoming more aware of happy feelings as they occur."

Keeping a Happiness List, either mentally or actually writing one, creates a tool which is one example of the concepts at work. It teaches us that we are responsible for our own happiness (or unhappiness), that we have a choice over how we experience life, in that we can either store good feelings inside or else hold on to the bad feelings, and that we have the power to change the way we react.

Because these tools work primarily with affect and imagery, they are not just a form of "positive thinking." Instead they aim at a fundamental change in how the self collects, stores, and reproduces experience.

Translating Theory Into Action: Creating Tools

The following tools translate into action the concepts we have been considering; they are best learned through directly experiencing them.[4]

Tool #1: Collecting Happiness

Make a list of five good things that happened each day, five things or events you feel good about, that left you feeling happy. Experience the event, feel the feelings, store it internally as a scene, write it down, and later recall it. Do this daily, either before going to sleep or else periodically throughout the day. Remember to look for good feelings, be conscious of them, and then record them. This tool teaches us to store the good feelings inside and helps us let go of bad feelings, particularly shame.

Tool #2: Collecting Adequacy/Pride

Make a list of five things you did in each day—accomplishments, activities, situations you handled—which pleased you. These ought to leave you feeling proud and satisfied with yourself. Experience the event, feel the feelings, store it internally as a scene, write it down, and later recall it. This is a way of learning how to collect and bank self-esteem: pride in self, valuing of self, esteem for self. We must remember to consciously give ourselves those feelings on a daily basis. Consider this a daily pride list which directly combats shame.

TOOL #3: POWERLESSNESS SCENE

Identify and then describe in writing a current situation of powerlessness. It can be in any sphere of life. Then identify and discuss your specific affective reactions during it. Finally, identify two choices for coping differently with that situation that could enable you to take back the power.

The Tools in Action:
Experiences From the Course

There is no right way of incorporating these tools into one's daily routine. Participants in the course will describe how they adapted the various tools and, ultimately, internalized each as a vital new process in their lives.

Rita voiced the following reactions to using the *happiness/adequacy* tools: "I'm getting much better at this, and do it fairly regularly. I've incorporated these lists into a larger log that I've been keeping for some time. I like the idea of banking because I find myself being conscious of a happy moment and think of adding it to the list, and then when a bad moment appears I am better able to remember the happy one. Knowing what really makes me happy motivates me to search these things out." Alice shared her experiences: "As I continue with my happiness/adequacy lists, I find myself getting into the habit of positive thinking. The difference is becoming striking to me. I sometimes purposely do this exercise *before* I try to study at night to dispel my discouragement and lack of confidence. I'm surprised at the difference it makes. I used to think these lists were trivial, but they've become a part of me. My sister and I have talked about making it a regular habit to share these lists with each other to help reinforce a positive attitude." Jim spoke next: "This is a very useful and often-used tool. I find it cheers me when I'm depressed and at the same time puts my day in perspective as I'm forced to review it. I know myself better after singling out the things that really make me feel good." Randy added: "It's helpful to see that everyday happiness is a lot of 'little' things rather than a big happening. I do these each day and it gets easier." Mary joined in: "I love this tool. I do it every night no matter how tired I am. I think it's really the key, or part of it, to conscious living since it makes me recall the events of the day and really own what happened. It lets me appreciate the little things which made me smile which might otherwise go unnoticed and unremembered." Cathy felt similarly: "I do this daily too. It's getting so I'm always keeping one eye open to spot things which I feel good about. I think it's helping me dwell less on the bad things which always used to bring me down." John shared his perception of the tool: "I do this mentally quite often—particularly on a day when things aren't going too well and I need to reverse my old depression spiral." Sarah rounded out the discussion: "I find myself looking for things that make me happy and focusing more on good things. I'm also realizing and appreciating things and people that make me happy. I have a brighter outlook and the tools to help me when things are bad." For these individuals, using the tools has created internal changes in both attitude and behavior, resulting in enhanced well-being.

Over time, the way particular tools are used may change. Sonja reported: "I've changed the way I use the happiness/adequacy lists. Before, I used to write them down at the end of the day, but I found that many hours after the event I didn't have much feeling left. Now I try to note each event and decide right on the spot that this is indeed an item for the happiness or adequacy list. Somehow, that has the impact of making the present moment more memorable. At the end of the day, I try to recall as many of the moments as I can."

Other participants shared varied reactions, like Ken: "I learned to look for and concentrate on the many good and positive things in my life—which more and more equalled or became more frequent than the bad." Rudy added: "I really liked collecting the five good things and storing them inside. It's so easy, sometimes, to be critical of everything and not find any good in anything. And it's more fun to find the happy things." Jean shared her experience: "I use this tool semi-regularly, usually when I take the time to write my experiences with the tools down on paper. I found this list most helpful in focusing on what's 'going right' rather than just on problems." Collecting and storing happiness shifts one's internal perspective, creating a different stance or posture toward life events.

Then discussion shifted to the *adequacy* tool which some clearly found more difficult though all eventually learned to find useful. Ken began: "This tool has been fairly easy to keep up on from week-to-week. It makes me very conscious of the focus being on my adequacy—not on my inadequacies." Jean commented: "I try to find even small areas of adequacy and build upon these. This is effective because I need to take time to see how I'm doing and give myself credit." Cathy joined in: "When I do a job, I often wonder if I could've done it different, but the fact I did it makes it adequate. I've been doing much more this way and have more confidence." Jennifer commented next: "It became clear to me how I was discounting things I did that I felt good about. It's helpful to consciously own those things." Mary chimed in: "Since I tend to downgrade myself, this helped me force myself to acknowledge things I could be proud of." Rudy laughed: "Well, I always make lists anyway. Now I feel even better when I cross accomplishments off it—one by one. I also find myself doing things sometimes I tend to avoid. I feel more assertive." Rita added a more serious note: "Reviewing the day and placing priorities on all activities puts my mind in an objective frame. Viewing day-to-day living in this light helps in solidifying feelings of worth." Diane offered a confirming view: "I have more respect for myself and even work toward being able to write down things on my list. It's also made me realize I have to do other things well in addition to school. I feel more competent." Pride in self, assertiveness, feelings of worth, and competence are the fruits of labors spent with this tool, collecting adequacy.

A tool which is difficult gradually becomes easier or else self-discovery enhances one's ability to use it, as the following example illustrates. Two weeks after the adequacy tool was first presented, Tina told us: "I'm having difficulty with this one. I do a lot of things adequately but they're the same things daily: cooking, cleaning, shopping. Maybe I don't understand the tool. The things I do now are often taken for granted and seem unimportant to my husband and me. I don't collect a lot of self-esteem from doing them. However, on days that I teach, do volunteer work, or counseling I feel great about myself and my abilities to do things well." Two weeks after that, Tina reported a change: "I learned last week in class that a lot of my self-esteem comes from others instead of from within me. This week I've been trying to change that. My adequacy list included things I did which helped others but also things I did which pleased *me,* even though no one else may have been aware of them. *I* was, and that's what counts. That made me feel a little special. I still need to work at this one. I've never collected and stored feelings like this before. It will take more time and practice to really reap the benefits." Tina discovered how dependent her own self-esteem had been on others. Now she had a viable tool for reversing this pattern, for developing an *inner* source of basic valuing of self.

Carol also voiced difficulty with the adequacy tool: "I think the primary reason it's difficult for me is that my life hasn't been very activity-filled lately. I'm not a student and have no job or career pursuits at this time. I see school and career as easy sources of performances that can be viewed as adequate. But I've tried to use the tool anyway. I think I define 'adequate' pretty strictly—more like 'very good' or 'above average.'" Clearly, how strictly we define adequacy will have a marked bearing on how often we allow ourselves to feel adequate. The same is true if adequacy is entirely attached to our performance in the world.

Adequacy does not have to be contingent on performance. We can learn to collect adequacy from the small events which happen day-by-day rather than looking for some momentous accomplishment. We need not expect to walk on water in order to feel fundamentally adequate about ourselves. There are even times when just getting through the day is a reason to feel adequate. Collecting general happiness and specific adequacy, if practiced consistently, will eventually become second-nature, thereby promoting psychological health and a competent self.

Developing a Competent Self

We have explored vital principles of competence. *Living consciously* is essential if we are ever to gain a sense of mastery either over ourselves or in our human relationships. Living consciously enables us to mediate and change what would otherwise be more automatic reactions. Through making conscious *choices* we take hold of our inner selves as well as the reins over our own lives. We become actors, not reactors, taking responsibility for our own happiness or unhappiness, for what we become in this world.

Living consciously and choice are two vital building blocks of competence. *Power* is a third. Insofar as we live consciously we are able to see our varied choices for coping with whatever situations are at hand. When we have choice, we are in a position of power. These concepts are translations of *responsibility* into action and reinforce one another, thereby enhancing effectiveness in living. Through living consciously from a position of personal power, we learn to build a competent self.

Psychological health depends on being able to experience power and effectively counteract shame. Self-esteem is a direct outgrowth of these twin capabilities.

CHAPTER 2

Identity: The Self's Relationship with the Self

We will now extend the work we have begun in certain new directions. We live in the world of people and things and must learn to navigate it with dignity and competence. Becoming a competent self involves several vital dimensions, each of which we will consider in turn. We must build as well as maintain inner security in the face of life's vicissitudes. We must know how to collect and store self-esteem within ourselves. We must build a satisfying inner relationship with ourselves, literally behaving toward ourselves as worthy and adequate beyond question. Finally, we must learn how to nurture ourselves, actively providing ourselves with caring. These are essential building blocks of psychological health.

Principles of Psychological Health

What does it mean to feel secure? One of the principal meanings of security is a sense of inner peace or safety. To feel secure within ourselves is to feel free from fear, doubt, or danger. The question before us is how do we accomplish this task.

Let us begin our inquiry by considering a series of propositions which lay the groundwork for psychological health. Consider these ideas as basic principles for living life. Together they build toward inner security, that wellspring of effectiveness in living. Each is a basic principle of psychological health. As we proceed, imagine each as a seed we are planting directly in the soil of the self.

Our first principle has already been discussed, namely, that we have a measure of *choice* over how we feel, react, and over how we face life. We have choice over just how hurt or angry we need become in a particular situation. Likewise, no one can reject us *unless* we have first agreed to feel rejected. There is always that vital corridor of choice between outer events and the *meanings* we attach to those events.

Second, we must learn not to give others the *power* to determine how we feel about ourselves. That power ought to reside solely within ourselves. Of course, we can consider the feedback of others, even their criticism of us, but *we* alone must decide whether it is true. Hence, we must not automatically take inside and believe the messages communicated by others. Instead, we need to build a flexible shield about us, protecting our inner self. Imagine considering the feedback or message while it is outside our shield. If we decide the message is true about us, we can take it inside. If it is not true, then we simply ignore it.

Third, one of the hardest tasks of all is to learn how to *affirm* ourselves from within. To affirm the self is to openly value the self. Our culture teaches us to value ourselves for what we do or accomplish in the world of other humans. How precarious this leaves us when defeats, failures, or rejections come our way as they inevitably will in the natural course of living. We must learn to value ourselves whether or not others do if we are to build security within. Instead of valuing ourselves only for what we *do,* we must learn how to value ourselves for who we *are* and how we live our lives. Times come upon us when it is especially urgent to value ourselves from within. Some years ago a man we know was turned down for promotion two years in a row. He had to learn how to value himself when many others obviously did not. Though he finally received that promotion, he painstakingly developed a capacity for self-affirmation which will carry him through future disappointments.

Fourth, we must never *question* our fundamental worth or adequacy. And, remember, it is *we* ourselves who put our worth or adequacy on the line. It is *we* alone who put it up for grabs. When we have begun to doubt ourselves, we must actively reaffirm our worth or adequacy from within. In so doing, inner security becomes restored. We must always *behave* toward ourselves as worthy and adequate beyond question. That fundamental sense of ourselves must be kept inviolate.

Fifth, we must learn how to stop internal comparisons of self with others. We live in a culture which teaches us to compare ourselves to one another. This comes through parents comparing one child either with a sibling or another. It comes through the peer group and school setting which encourage being "better than" or seeking one's advantage over others—competitiveness in its varied forms. It also is transmitted through the media which bombard us with messages about what we ought to look like, dress like, think and be like. Because our culture generally does not recognize and value individual differences, we fail to learn to do so for ourselves. Comparison making usually opens a trap-door over the whirlpool of shame and doubt. We are left feeling deficient or lesser for the comparison and our security is eroded. We can stop these invidious comparisons by saying, "I will not talk to myself like this—we are *different*." We can thus learn how to value our essential human differences, affirming the unique self we are.

Sixth, equally vital is learning not to attach our inner feelings of worth or adequacy to externals, or to anything that happens to us in the world. This means we must be able to fail at something without having to feel like a failure as a person. Hence, the external event ceases being a statement about our intrinsic worth. Whether or not we receive a desired promotion, raise, or position is not a measure of our inherent adequacy. Likewise, whether a particular relationship works or fails must not automatically attach to our inner sense of worth or adequacy. Both our worth and adequacy need to be kept separate from whatever happens to us in the world.

Seventh, we fare better in life when we invest emotionally in those endeavors which are in our control. For example, we are fully invested in writing this book; that we have full control over. But whether a publisher deems it worthy of publishing is quite another matter. We cannot invest in publishing it to the same extent as we are invested in writing it because we lack full control over the publishing end of it. Likewise, if it does get published, we cannot invest in how widely it is read because, again, we do not have the control over it. Another example. We are fully invested in how we teach our courses; these are in our control. But whether we advance either in our career or else in the organization for which we work are beyond our full control.

Eighth, remember that life is a mixed bag and happiness is a by-product of living. So many of us have been raised with the expectation that we *should* be happy, that something was wrong if we were not. Happiness is not a goal to be striven for, but more like a feather floating on the breeze. Grasping for it will simply push it further from us. A more realistic expectation is that if we are happy fifty percent of the time, then we are doing really well! And, remember, there are bad months, even bad years, from time to time. The fairy tales told to children about "living happily ever after" are, unfortunately, insufficiently countered by a healthy dose of reality. Children who are fed only the tales are ill-prepared for living life. They grow up expecting to be happy and suffer greatly because their expectations are not matched to reality as it inevitably is. And when the truth finally dawns, how deceived we feel.

Ninth, we are each fully responsible for our own happiness. No one else can *make* us happy. Others can *care* about our happiness, certainly, but we must enhance it. We have full choice over how we face life and experience ourselves. That is our inheritance as human beings, to make what we will of ourselves.

Tenth, we must actively keep alert for situations in which we feel powerless and/or trapped. The two together can be devastating. A situation in which we feel powerless and trapped, particularly when extended over time, can potentially erode mental health. Powerlessness is an activator of negative affect and one of the most pervasive sources of shame. Extended powerlessness produces overwhelming shame. One of the clearest examples of this was universally witnessed: the "Hostage Crisis" in Iran. That was a prime example of a situation in which a group of individuals were both powerless and trapped over an extended period of time. An entire nation experienced an analogous sense of powerlessness, shame, and rage. Powerlessness can be experienced with any negative affect or combination thereof, including shame, contempt, rage, fear, or distress (crying). Rage is a frequent reaction to powerlessness. The experience of being powerless and trapped is a profoundly regressive one which erodes mental health because it violates security. Powerlessness experienced during adulthood reactivates the scene of infant helplessness which we then relive in the present. What is necessary is consciously identifying and naming these feelings. Then we must observe the situation to see our realistic choices for taking back the power. We can always take back the power within ourselves either by changing our attitude, changing our expectations, or by detaching from the situation.

Eleventh, we must learn how to maintain equal power in our human relationships whenever realistically possible. We will examine this at greater length later when we consider relationships more fully. The goal we are aiming for is *equal* power, not power *over* others. We aim to share the power in a relationship but never to relinquish our rightful half of the power.

Twelfth, we must also learn how to build a network of *security relationships* because it is not sufficient to build security only within. Until the turn of the century, the extended family served this purpose. There existed a support network of significant individuals surrounding the family which enabled many to maintain security even in the worst life events. We no longer have such a functioning network in our culture, in part owing to our increasing societal mobility. We create security in the world through building security relationships: those few, special individuals to whom we look for our basic human needs. There are times when we need others to care for us, support us, and value us. We need at least one, and preferably two or three, security relationships. How to build these relationships will be explored in depth later.

The foregoing twelve principles are a foundation of psychological health.

Collecting and Storing Self-Esteem

Through making *Happiness Lists* and *Adequacy Lists,* as described earlier, we teach ourselves how to collect both general happiness and more specific pride in self. The next step is "banking" these feelings and memories inside of us. Imagine accumulating internal bank accounts of *Happiness* and *Adequacy,* by storing items or events from our lists. Many individuals begin each day at *zero* rather than carry over feelings of happiness or adequacy from previous days. This does not leave us well prepared for the disasters of life.

If we accumulate these deposits of happiness and adequacy, we can draw against them in the hard times or bad times. Then when we blunder, we can draw against a surplus of good feelings and memories. If we make a costly mistake on a particular occasion, we can consciously remind ourselves of the situations handled well over the preceding days or week. Thereby, accumulated small successes can offset failures.

Furthermore, we have an inalienable right to make a mistake. Never do we function consistently at our best. We are human and imperfect and might as well accept that fact, even rejoice in it. We ought to *expect* to behave stupidly and clumsily, lacking good judgment, some of the time. That is an inevitable part of our nature as people. Though we did not use to, we now *expect* to make mistakes on a daily basis, mistakes of judgment. Expecting to make significant mistakes at least four times a day is more realistic than expecting to never make mistakes.

Consider the following incident related by a student in the course: "I was hurrying to get my delivery men going on a refrigerator delivery that had to be delivered before 9:30 a.m. I discovered after they were gone that I had them load the wrong model. I felt good that I could tell myself I still had 'three big mistakes' to go—for my daily allotment! I still like the idea of allowing myself four big mistakes each day. I can feel good if I don't use them all. If I do go over, I can fall back on my bank account of good and adequacy feelings."

Clearly, in order to collect self-esteem, we must have a means to do so. The bank account metaphor provides a tool for accomplishing that. We also must hold expectations of ourselves that are more in keeping with reality.

Creating a Self-Affirming Inner Relationship with Ourselves

Being a self in the world is no easy task. Being the best possible self one can be is even harder. It means fully accepting the person one is and rejoicing in it. To accept our failings and weaknesses, our human imperfections, is to reclaim once-hated parts, to heal our inner strife, and so become whole. A self divided cannot endure.

When we have grown up with shame, we learn to shame ourselves, and thereby feel divided within. We reproduce shame through the actual ways we behave towards ourselves.

The central idea is that we learn to relate to ourselves in certain characteristic ways just as we learn to do so with others. Each of us has an active relationship with ourselves. Not only do we have thoughts and feelings about ourselves, but more importantly, we adopt particular attitudes toward ourselves and learn to treat ourselves accordingly. Usually we learn to treat ourselves precisely the way we were treated growing up by significant others, unless we work to change it. Through the moment-to-moment actions taking place inside our skins, we behave toward the self inside of us either respectfully, tenderly, or else, as is too often the case, rather critically.

One way this inner relationship manifests is through the actual ways we converse with ourselves. Often we find an inner voice inside which whispers either support or criticism. Many of us have learned to *blame* ourselves when things go wrong in life. Or we have learned to *compare* ourselves to others and feel deficient for the comparison. Or else we have learned to be critical, actively *contemptuous* towards ourselves, resulting in splits within us. Is it any wonder, then that we so often end up feeling inadequate, deficient, or depressed? Later we will examine other examples of divisions within the self.

These divisions manifest through the relationship we form and actively carry on with ourselves. As children, we *identify* with our parents or others who become special to us, and we seek to become like them. No wish of the child is greater than to be like the deeply loved or needed parent who is central in the child's world. Identification is a visual process and we identify through observational learning. What we see and observe then transfers inside the self through the medium of visual imagery. The inner process of seeing visual images or pictures in the mind's eye mediates the transfer from outer to inner. What is first experienced or observed outside the self is taken inside, or internalized, through identification. The *internal image* then forms the basis for the evolving relationship which the self comes to have with the self.

Consider the following example. If a girl grows up in a blaming family, then naturally occurring mistakes or failings, which are to be expected in the course of daily living, are met with blame. A girl living in a blaming environment has no other *model* for having a relationship with herself and so will internalize an image of the blaming parent. That internal image sets the inner stage for how she will later behave toward herself in like instances. Future occasions of mistaken judgment will reactivate that internal blaming image and the self then continues the identical pattern of blaming the self for mistakes, a pattern first learned in the family. We learn to treat ourselves precisely the way we were treated growing up by significant others. This pattern is the basis of our inner relationship and underlies our evolving identity.

It must also be remembered that we live in a culture infested with blame. As soon as anything goes wrong, attention is focused upon discovering who was to blame: someone must be found responsible. Certainly there is a useful aspect to this whole business of fault-finding; perhaps we might learn how to avert similar mishaps. Yet this is not the point, at least not entirely so. The blame must be fixed somewhere so that all others associated with the event can wash their hands of it and feel innocent. It is this *transfer of blame* for inevitable mistakes which is so insidious in our culture.

Creating a self-affirming inner relationship with ourselves is essential to supporting inner security and self-esteem. To create such a relationship translates into behaving toward ourselves as worthy and adequate beyond question. Accomplishing this task means consciously changing the ways we both converse with and treat ourselves. We must become conscious of the inner patterns we actively engage in which either support and affirm the self or else reproduce shame through *self-blame, self-contempt,* and *comparison-making.*

OBSERVING INNER VOICES

We must work to recognize our inner relationship by *observing* our typical ways of behaving toward ourselves in various situations. Imagine the following situations and your usual inner voices.

First, when you get up in the morning and look at yourself in the mirror, what do you say? Do you speak kindly or critically?

Second, when you have blundered, failed, or made a serious mistake of judgment how do you speak to yourself? Do you berate yourself for having made the mistake in the first place? Are we not human and entitled to make mistakes? Must we blame ourselves for being imperfect?

Third, how do you speak to yourself when you have done well at some venture in life or accomplished something of value? Do you give yourself real feelings of pride in self or do you puncture your self-esteem by fault-finding: "I could've done this better—it wasn't good enough."

Fourth, does anger sit well with you or instead frighten itself away? Do you become filled with regret or guilt and punish yourself for reacting angrily toward someone? How do you respond to your wrath, especially after a fight with a friend, parent, or spouse?

Fifth, after talking to someone in a position of authority, whether a teacher or a supervisor at work, do you speak disparagingly to yourself or respectfully?

Sixth, when you leave any *new* interpersonal situation, do you find fault with how you came across or handled yourself? Do you replay all of the things you could have done better? Do you compare yourself with those strangers and feel the lesser?

Seventh, when you leave the home of a valued friend, do you feel comforted or nurtured? Are you critical of what transpired, poking holes in yourself at any opportunity?

Eighth, following a visit or phone call with your parents, do you feel pleasure in the contact, disappointment, or anger? Do you behave tenderly and respectfully toward yourself or with contempt or blame?

Ninth, consider how you speak to yourself when someone pays you a compliment or says, "I like you." Can you receive it well, feeling pleasure in the gift, or must you feel unworthy, undeserving, or ashamed?

Tenth, when someone you know well disappoints you, how do you respond to your hurt? Do you own these feelings or reject them? Or do you mask them with rage?

Eleventh, when you have disappointed someone special, do you blame yourself or feel contempt in response? Do you openly acknowledge the situation and your role in it, recognizing that sometimes you will be a disappointment to others? Or do you do anything to avoid another's disappointment, and in so doing, give up what matters most to your essential self?

Twelfth, and finally, there are times when we all feel somewhat young, needy, or otherwise insecure. How do you speak to yourself at such moments? Are you tender and loving or disgusted and critical? How we speak to ourselves at these moments determines whether inner security becomes restored or further ruptured.

When we become conscious of our characteristic ways of relating to ourselves, those inner voices we live with, then we are in a position to actively work toward changing them. We can change these moment-to-moment inner voice patterns away from anger, blame, contempt, or criticism directed toward the self and replace them with respect, tenderness, valuing of self, and forgiveness for mistakes and failings. To accomplish such a change requires consistent conscious effort over time. While we will certainly see tangible though smaller gains more quickly, such relearning will likely take a year or more to become second-nature. We will never become perfect at it, but replacing inner voices is learnable. The process involves first observing the contemptuous, blaming, or comparing voice; next recovering the governing scene in which the voice is rooted by visualizing the voice; then creating a new voice with new words, new feelings, and a new image; finally imagine someone older who respects you actually speaking the new words inside. This completes the process because it directly engages imagery in replacing a shaming voice with a self-affirming one. All three processes have to be directly engaged: *affect, imagery,* and *language*.

Let us consider several course experiences with discovering and changing inner voices. Alice spoke first: "The negative voice in me has been my habitual way of 'whipping' myself into shape. Now that I realize what a vicious circle I get myself into with self-condemnation, I'm trying hard to encourage, forgive, be kind to myself, even laugh with myself. The kind voices sometimes have to scream and yell to crowd out the negative—but they are coming through." Ken picked up the thought: "I've found that I can change my moods, calm myself down, and make decisions easier by first becoming conscious of present thoughts and, then, deliberately changing them to a more constructive form." Helen agreed: "I have been much more forgiving of myself. I try to converse with myself from the vantage point of later perspective, like, will it matter ten years from now the mistakes I make today." Carmen provided an example of her usual inner voice: "What I often say to myself is this, 'You ass! I can't believe I said that. What did I just do? Oh, my God.' I'm learning to jump back and listen to myself; sometimes I slap my hand but mostly I'm learning to forgive myself and move on." These individuals were learning to actively change their inner voices in ways which promote self-respect, valuing and forgiveness, and counter shame.

DEVELOPING AN INTERNAL SENSE OF HOW MUCH IS GOOD ENOUGH

Replacing our inner voices is one dimension of creating a new relationship with ourselves. An equally important dimension is developing an internal sense of how much is *good enough* rather than striving for perfection. Our culture teaches us to measure our inner sense of worth or adequacy according to our accomplishments. The more we accomplish and the better we do in our pursuits, the better we are allowed to feel about ourselves. In this way, self-esteem becomes contingent upon our performance or achievement in the world. Perfectionism is a treadmill: we must excel in an ever-widening circle of activities.

The cultural admonition that "anything worth doing is worth doing well" robs us of *choice*. Some things are worth doing simply for pleasure, such as bicycling, swimming, music, and crafts. We do not have to become proficient or accomplished at all endeavors. We must consciously set our own expectations of ourselves in each and every sphere of life, in order to develop an internal sense of how much is good enough.

This translates, for example, into choosing just what level of grade one wishes to work for in a particular course. We need not feel obligated always to do our best at all things. Choosing to work for a lower grade is just as valid as working for a top grade. There are certainly consequences; one may need to excel to gain admission to professional school. But knowing we have a choice, and living from a position of choice, frees us from perfectionism.

Dennis felt crippled by severe anxiety spirals which centered around his academic performance. He had recently returned to school and to him anything less than an "A" meant failure. He would approach each exam with fear and trembling because he absolutely had to make an "A" each time, or else he felt horribly inadequate. Anything less than perfect was altogether unacceptable. His inner sense of adequacy was inextricably tied to his external performance; when one fell so did the other. His entire self-worth as a useful, contributing individual was predicated on his continuing to achieve and excel. Dennis needed to separate his inner sense of worth and adequacy from his external performance. Once he was able to recognize the emotional price he was paying for his unrealistic expectations of himself, he could gradually begin to relinquish the need to be perfect. Dennis even felt rather pleased one day when his lower grade had matched his consciously lowered expectations.

Consider another example. Sonja, a woman in our course, reported that after joining Phi Kappa Phi, she found out the required grade point average was 3.98. She became scared, wondering if she now would have to *maintain* that kind of standard in all areas. Sonja was able to change her attitude by consciously deciding it was okay to have a variety of abilities in different areas. She did not have to do equally well in everything.

Finally, Bill kept a vegetable garden in the summertime for relaxation. His goal was to enjoy the process of growing things, not to become good at it. It was all too easy, however, for Bill to forget the reasons he was gardening and feel impelled to turn it into another job to be done well. We need not become competent at all our activities. We actually pay a price unless we consciously keep some for enjoyment or pleasure.

We maximize choice and enhance power by deciding for ourselves how much is good enough in each and every activity we engage in. We all have an inalienable right to waste our potential. Whose potential is it anyway?

DISTINGUISHING THE SOURCES OF GUILT/SHAME

The experience commonly known as guilt has not been accurately understood, according to Silvan Tomkins who made the critical observation that:

> "shyness in the presence of a stranger, shame at a failure and guilt for a transgression or immorality were, *at the level of affect,* phenomenologically one and the same affect. Different components in the three experiences along with shame are what make them feel so distinctly different. Here, guilt can be understood as feeling disappointed in oneself for violating an important internal value or code of behavior. Shame over a failure also feels like a disappointment in self. But here no value has been violated; one has simply failed to cope with a challenge. The meaning of the two experiences is as different as feeling inadequate is from feeling immoral. But in each experience, one still feels bad as a person; the head hangs low.
>
> "When we are concerned with this dimensional quality of inner experience, it makes little difference to distinguish shame from guilt. The *affect* is still the same in each and the affect is the principal component of the overall experience."[1]

Tomkins now defines guilt as *immorality shame*. Much that has been traditionally labeled as guilt is, on closer inspection, internalized contempt; this is in addition to immorality shame. Many of us learn to treat ourselves with contempt or else to blame ourselves when things go wrong. Usually when someone describes a feeling of guilt, either self-blame or self-contempt is an additional contributing source.

One further distinction must be drawn. In a sense, we can think of two sources of guilt. The first is *disappointing self* while the other is *disappointing others*. For example, guilt is frequently triggered when someone wants something of us which we do not want to do. We learn to feel guilty about saying "no" through previous interactions with significant others who have reacted with hurt when we have said "no." These are instances of disappointing others. Whenever faced with a choice between disappointing ourselves or disappointing someone else in any essential matter, it is preferable to disappoint the other.

There are countless times in the course of life when the needs of individuals in a relationship will conflict. Then we must take stock of ourselves to know whether acceding to the other's need or request will mean significantly disappointing ourselves. How we handle these situations depends on the importance of the relationship, nature of the request or situation, our own pressing needs at that particular juncture, and what we really do have to give at that point. Whenever we feel guilty, we must honestly ask ourselves: "Am I feeling guilty because I am disappointing myself or because I am disappointing someone else?" Distinguishing between these is the principal tool for guiding our actions wisely.

Self-Nurturance and Self-Forgiveness

Our next consideration involves learning how to actively care for ourselves, literally how to *nurture* the self inside of us. It is essential that we cultivate tangible ways of nurturing ourselves. Buying oneself a present is one example. Taking oneself out someplace special, to a movie or out to dinner, is another way of actively nurturing the self. Giving oneself time alone when that is needed is another way of caring for the self. We must cultivate ways of nurturing ourselves.

Consider the following comments from Jean: "I used to think that I was supposed to be productive all of the time and that spending time on *me* was a waste. Now that I'm learning to feel better about myself, I recognize the importance of nurturing myself and don't feel guilty. I am much better at forgiving myself." Helen had this to say: "Amidst all the activity I seem to get involved in, this tool reminds me of the activities that give me the greatest joy in living." Mary discovered tangible ways of nurturing herself: "A hot bath when cold or tired or sad; reading something 'just for me;' seeking out someone's company when lonely; writing a letter." Each of these individuals began learning the importance of self-nurturance in promoting psychological health.

We do not work well for long-delayed gratification. Instead we must remember to build in tangible rewards on a daily or weekly basis. These give us something to work for and look forward to. Following real disappointments and losses, we must be especially tender towards ourselves and find ways to heal the inner wound.

When we have done some regrettable deed or committed some wrongdoing, however grievous, we must find a way to wipe the slate clean and forgive ourselves for it. For every wrongdoing there is a punishment and a statute of limitations. There must come a time when we again embrace ourselves, deciding we have suffered enough: "It is time to forgive myself." Atonement for a wrongdoing is, at a deeper level, a return to a state of *at-onement* with oneself. To forgive oneself is to return to that state of inner wholeness, reunion with with oneself. By forgiving ourselves for our most imperfect humanness, we become *one* with ourselves again and, in so doing, become whole.

True nurturance of self embraces caring and forgiveness.

Temperament Patterns

Psychological health is founded on certain premises, not the least of which is full recognition and acceptance of one's unique nature as a self. There are recognizable temperament patterns, such as introversion or extroversion, which probably are biologically given. Nature endows us with specific temperaments which nevertheless remain open to modification through learned experience. Though pure types are by no means the rule, it is useful to identify these temperament patterns because they are inherent to the self.

Certain individuals are predisposed toward extroversion. These people are socially oriented, require interaction, are more freely verbal, and more outgoing. Their interest is directed outward. Verbalizing comes easily to the extrovert who thrives on verbal interaction. To think out a problem, the extrovert may need to verbalize it to another individual. Thinking itself can become externalized.

Introverted individuals are usually quieter, harder to know and less socially oriented. Their interest is predominantly directed inward. Introverts require less human interaction. Introverts do not have to *verbalize* their inner experience: they prefer to think out problems internally.

Each of us must learn to understand our own intrinsic nature, how we literally function as a self. We must learn to accept and value either our inherent introvertedness or extrovertedness rather than seek to be different from the self we are.

Another aspect of temperament is the tendency toward cycloid mood swings which appears to occur in conjunction with extroversion. The introvert is not typically given to cycloid mood swings but, rather, to becoming more or less withdrawn. The extrovert-cycloid temperament combination tends to cycle *up and down* while the introvert usually moves *in and out*.

Innate temperament differences will influence how we experience and respond to life events, including threatening or stressful ones. One style is not better than the other; they are simply *different*. The central point is that temperament is a vital aspect of the self which requires conscious awareness.

Sexual Orientation

Just as temperament is a product of both innate and learned factors, sexual orientation is the result of an interaction among innate, prenatal, and environmental influences. We cannot experience psychological health if we refuse to acknowledge and accept our sexual orientation when it is rejected by the culture in which we live. Gays, lesbians, and bisexuals face a host of obvious as well as unspoken cultural and religious prohibitions and sanctions which readily become sources of shame connected to their inherent nature. Psychological health and self-esteem require that we actively embrace and openly value our differentness as individuals—especially when that differentness expresses our loving and sexual natures.

When the disparaging, shaming, and accusatory voices of our culture become internalized, and thereby mistaken as one's own voice, our resulting inner voices reproduce shame through self-blame and self-contempt targeted at being gay or lesbian. Then we grow to hate, repudiate, and torment ourselves, as if attempting to squash, distance, or rid ourselves of contamination. Because the judged contaminant is inherent to our nature, inevitably we are at war with ourselves. This is what homophobia actually is: shame and contempt directed at being gay.

In this culture, people of difference, whether sexual or otherwise, struggle to maintain their self-esteem because their very difference itself contributes to their sense of powerlessness and feeling outcast. In this acute dilemma, openly valuing oneself, resisting invidious comparisons with others, and keeping our fundamental sense of worth and adequacy beyond question become both more urgent and more difficult.

The Self as an Evolving Integration: The Inner Child

As development proceeds from childhood through adolescence into adulthood, the self evolves through a series of discrete phases. Imagine the self as a collection of selves, including the earliest *child-self* all the way up to the most mature phase to which the self has evolved. The task toward which development impels us is one of *integrating* these earlier phases of the self into a unified whole.

Life events can trigger reactions on many levels, from adult to child. We must know when we are reacting from a younger level in order to know how best to grow beyond it. Life events which render us powerless as adults in any significant sphere will likely activate the child-self inside us, occasioning a massive intrusion of early experience. We need to consciously recognize when we are reacting from a young level and we need to nurture that child within us when it has surfaced.

We must experience and consciously integrate the child-self in order to restore security. One way is through communicating with our inner child, comfortingly and reassuringly. We need to behave toward our inner child with tenderness and respect, treating that little boy or girl inside of us precisely the way a scared, insecure child needs. This inner response restores security.

Talking to oneself as if one were two people must seem like a rather strange notion, yet along that path lies eventual integration. Through actively nurturing our inner child we are gradually able to restore security, inner peace, and safety. An example of this would be setting aside time for the child part of us to get some needs met.

One man, Ken, became fully conscious of the inner child within him and began learning how to nurture this vital part of him. One day he was browsing through the toy department and stopped to admire the model railroad sets. All at once, the little boy inside him said, "I want that." Then he said to himself, "Okay, little kid, I'll buy you the train set." He did, set up the model railroad in his basement, and spent long hours after work playing with his trains. That became a real way of nourishing and eventually integrating this part of him. Over many months he learned to restore security within and eventually integrate his inner child as one distinguishable part of an integrated self. He was finally able to put that child to rest in a safe place inside.

Another man, Peter, gradually contacted his inner child. Once it became fully conscious, he was able to discover ways of caring for the little boy within him. Peter had always wanted a teddy bear. After receiving one from a valued friend, Peter had the courage to buy himself others he admired. Talking to his bears and holding them became a viable way of actively nourishing his inner child, thereby restoring security.

In the course, Carol reported: "The little girl inside me wanted to go kite-flying last weekend. We did, along with some other friends, and had a great time." Rudy told us: "I find myself talking to my child during the course of my day. I tell him, 'Let's do this task and I'll reward you later.' It helps me to not avoid things I need to get done."

Bobbi reported trouble concentrating on working with her inner child. Talking with a good friend at a party helped her share her loneliness, and she ended up feeling so secure afterwards that she wanted to try that with her inner child. She went back to a humiliating incident that occurred when she was nine years old. She told her best friend that she had a crush on one of the boys in their class. The friend stood up and announced it, and Bobbi was teased unmercifully. Coming home in tears, she found her mother too busy and uninterested to give her the comfort and empathy she needed, so she just crawled into her closet and curled up into a ball in the corner.

Remembering this scene, she imagined her adult self crawling in there and holding her child while she cried. Then she took the child's hand, led her out to sit on the bed and read her a story. They talked for a while, and then the little girl was ready to go outside and play. "It was very freeing to relive that experience and comfort my inner child," Bobbi told us. "I've called up that little girl since then whenever I feel like I want to curl up into a ball in the closet, and it allows me to feel comforted every time."

Each of these individuals discovered a vital child-self within them as adults, and further learned how to actively care for that inner child.

The self is not comprised of discrete *states,* but is rather a *process* involving conscious differentiation followed by integration. The self evolves through a series of developmental phases much as a tree adds rings of growth. Each successive phase or ring remains potentially within awareness. Earlier phases of self remain essential parts of us throughout adulthood and are either partially conscious already or else available to consciousness. The task is one of differentiating each phase of self, making it fully conscious, and finally integrating them. The image of the self unfolding here is one of an evolving integration. Moving toward an ever-more differentiated and integrated self is the natural course of development.

Translating Theory Into Action:
Creating Tools

TOOL #1: BECOMING CONSCIOUS OF AND CHANGING
OUR INNER VOICES

Be conscious of the ways you typically converse with yourself inside, particularly following disappointments, mistakes, and failings. Then consciously try to change the way you behave toward yourself *away from* anger, self-blame, contempt, or criticalness, *toward* respect, tenderness, valuing of self, and forgiveness for mistakes and failings.

TOOL #2: CULTIVATING WAYS OF NURTURING SELF

Set aside some time in every day to actively nourish and care for yourself, some activity that directly nurtures you inside either at the adult or child level. This is a way of learning to care for ourselves.

TOOL #3: REPARENTING IMAGERY[2]

Close your eyes and call up an image of the young boy or girl you were around either age five or age ten, whichever comes easiest to mind. Beginning with happier memories, try to visualize that child as clearly as possible: see how you dressed, your way of walking or skipping, and your mannerisms. When you have a clear, vivid image of the child you were back then, ask your child to come over, sit beside you, and hold your hand. Now talk to that child, asking about feelings and needs. Then be the good parent or older friend to your child you wish you had had. Before you complete this experience, imagine giving that child a great big hug and tucking your child into bed, in a new, safe place, as if somewhere inside of you.

If you have difficulty, find a photograph of yourself at that age, look at it awhile, and then enter the imagery.[3]

The Tools in Action:
Experiences From the Course

Working to make conscious and then change our *inner voices* challenges individuals who desire a more satisfying inner relationship with themselves. In the course, Barbara spoke about her recent experience using the tool: "I got upset with myself this week because I can't be more like a friend of mine in talking more freely with people. I told myself to stop it, that I'm a *different* person and it helped." Jean chimed in: "Yes, when I found myself comparing me with two friends, I stopped and said we are different people. It was very helpful." Rudy observed: "It's very illuminating when I catch myself deprecating myself. I notice it a lot in others too. I seem to catch myself after I've already criticized myself. I'm not sure yet how to *prevent* negative self-dialogue. Ironically, I'll criticize myself for criticizing myself." A week later, Rudy reported: "I've started talking to my inner child when he's scared or wants to give up on something. This helps even out my feelings. Also, at times when I do something that's really stupid or embarrassing, I remind myself that I'm granted several screwups in a day and I actively forgive myself. This really helps the stupid feeling pass." Jim shared his reactions to the tool: "I'm trying, as situations arise, to stop talking negatively to myself before things even happen and instead focus on what other people are doing, how they appear, etc. I'm trying to accept myself as I am now, instead of always griping about what I can't do or haven't done." A week later, Jim added: "I don't yell at myself anymore. If I can't say something nice or objective, I don't say anything to myself."

Others had more difficulty with the tool. Tina said: "I've just started to really listen to my inner voices. It's hard for me to change a negative message to myself into a positive one. If I've made a mistake, well then I've made one, but I'm often more understanding and forgiving of others than I am towards myself. I'm not doing so well, but I'm working on this one." Two weeks later, Tina reported: "I'm making some progress towards talking to myself with respect and tenderness, even though I have a difficult time forgiving myself if I've made the same mistake before."

Change is a conscious, effortful process requiring practice over time, as Tina's experience illustrates. It takes patience and determination to unlearn an old pattern and replace it with a new one. Certain people will alter the tool to suit their unique self. Steve made the following variation: "I find inner voices more useful as a written exercise. First, when I'm getting down on myself or others, I ask, 'What am I expecting of myself or them and how realistic are these expectations?' Then I write out my thoughts and feelings as they were first occurring, my actual inner voice. Next I rewrite them, taking into account how realistic my expectations are."

When discussion shifted to the *self-nurturance* tool, one of the themes which surfaced was how undeserving many individuals had felt. Alice remarked: "I used to have myself convinced there was practically nothing I needed or wanted. My whole life was one of making do with what came my way. Now that I'm getting in touch with what I want and need, depression lifts, but real frustration and anger usually replace it because I don't have the means to get what I want. I'm cultivating patience with myself and taking simple steps one at a time." Tina shared her difficulties with self-nurturance: "I believe that one of the many reasons I may have become ill was because I didn't nurture myself during a very stressful time in my life. Everyone else's needs and desires came first. I felt selfish if I wanted something just to give me pleasure. That's changed now. I now feel special enough to treat myself well. I'm doing at least one thing a day I truly enjoy."

Others shared their experiences with the tool. Jim was first. "I respect myself, care for myself, and accept myself more. I'm treating myself as a friend. All of this has helped me be less hard on myself." Diane chimed in: "Doing nice things for myself—I can't believe that I actually had to be *told* to do that! At any rate, I'm glad I was, if that's what it took—everyone deserves feeling worthwhile." Sarah joined the discussion: "I wish I could find ways to nurture myself besides eating! The lack of time in my life doesn't allow for much opportunity to give myself treats that involve doing things. There's one exception. I allow myself some time, almost every day, for exercise—running, swimming, ballet—these are treats." Rita offered other examples: "I've been willing to make some financial investments, for example, buying 'one-only' items such as place settings or liqueur glasses." Irene commented: "I didn't go to work today—I felt I needed a day off." Carol rounded out the discussion: "One day I took a walk by the river. It gave me time to rejuvenate and it felt wonderful. On another day I took myself out for ice cream and also listened to a song I've always wanted to hear. I deserved this and it felt good."

Discussion shifted to the theme of self-forgiveness. Rhoda began: "This is a tough one for me. I don't feel I deserve to forgive myself. It's hard. Like I always have to be paying for my past mistakes. And as long as I'm doing that, I can't treat myself right." Judy agreed: "Forgiveness has never been easy or possible for me. I haven't been able to forgive myself, or sometimes others, for past wrongs and shortcomings. But I'm trying to work on it—at least I'm finally aware of it." Arthur commented: "Forgiveness is big—there's release here. We must also forgive our parents for their incompleteness and for being less than we wanted and expected. I'm continuing to discover the significance in forgiving myself and others."

Learning to nurture ourselves, to care for and forgive ourselves, is a vital tool for living competently. Many individuals in our culture have not learned this; either they feel guilty or else undeserving. Self-nurturance embraces a principle of living which requires cultivation.

When we moved to consider *reparenting imagery,* one of the themes which surfaced repeatedly was reparenting and healing the self. Carmen was first: "Conjuring up my child self and being kind and reassuring to her was personally very useful. I've always felt neglected by my mother. I was a middle child, quiet, undemanding. Guess who got the attention? So—just saying kind things to myself as a child has made me feel much better." Robert commented: "I found myself wishing I could have been my own father." Stuart added: "This is a neat way of learning to accept yourself, how you were, and how you became what you are." Jennifer responded with: "I enjoy helping my inner child and I'm starting to learn where I came from. I feel sorry for the lonely child inside me. I want to reassure her and make her happy. I feel motherly, protective."

Laura said: "The most powerful experience I had was going back to my inner child. She asked me why I was always trying so hard. I hugged her and told her she didn't have to try so hard, that I would love her no matter what she did or didn't do. But that night I had this nightmare of reaching for a rope that was always just beyond my hands. When I woke up, really upset, I used imagery to picture my inner child and that rope. I told her to sit down because she was tired. She was so relieved and content not to have to keep struggling!"

Alice joined the discussion: "I use this task only occasionally, but when I do I find it a powerful experience. I'm using it to reprogram some attitudes I developed early in my life. I find it a freeing experience to give that child in me permission to spread her wings."

Tina had a parallel experience over several weeks: "I need to do this one more often. The times I've done it have been extremely helpful in healing past hurts. Using this tool is causing a deep inner healing which I didn't believe possible. At times I have very frightening memories, but while I'm reparenting myself, I can stop the traumatic things from happening and that in itself is healing. Being the 'good' and 'loving' and 'protective' parent I always wanted and didn't have by far has been the most healing and freeing."

Frightening or painful feelings are often experienced through this particular tool, as Tina also observed. Judy said: "I tried it again and it really worked well. Last time I tried it, I cried, but this time it was a warm feeling." Rhoda added: "This tool scares me the most but has given me the most insight into me. I still haven't gotten over the intensity of the newly understood feelings to find a way to deal with or satisfy my child needs. Using this tool is beginning to be a more positive experience. I haven't yet figured out how to satisfy her needs, but I've learned what they are."

Rita reported the following reactions over a three-week period: "When you first asked us to do this in the class, I had extreme difficulty emotionally (not rationally) doing it and I stopped midway. I'm curious as to why since I didn't think this would be hard. . . . I'm still inching towards this one. I hold safe conversations with the kid, but I sense that some sort of a shell still exists for self-preservation. I can respect the boundaries at this point. I'm sure there is a good reason. . . . I'm getting more involved with this one but it's like an onion that's being peeled layer by layer."

Experiences with the tool are rich and varied indeed; consider Sonja's: "This has been most surprising. The child I contact is so different from my ordinary conscious self. She is full of surprises. I never know from day-to-day how she will be or what will happen in our imaginary interactions. . . . We went for a walk in the woods during the day. In the evening, my inner child told me she liked it very much and that it would have been even better if I had not occasionally been thinking about problems during the walk. . . . Today I imagined myself at age twelve—a time which was not at all good for me. I got sad and depressed for a whole day afterwards, but also realized how some of my present feelings stem from that period. . . . Getting in touch with my inner child is very useful. It seems as if my child is sometimes giving me advice like, 'Don't take that so seriously' or 'Together we'll figure something out.' "

Utilizing reparenting imagery is a powerful tool for recontacting painful and even traumatic scenes in childhood, even occasionally scenes of physical or sexual abuse. Some individuals who are not ready to reexperience these events will either go to sleep, resist the imagery, or experience disruptions during it. Others will enter the scene and then consciously stop it, experiencing a reluctance or dread of continuing further. These are self-protective mechanisms that enable one to only reenter the scene when one is fully ready to recover and reexperience it. This imagery should never be required, forced, or expected. One should always respect one's readiness to recover scenes and reexperience them. Some people will enter the imagery and unexpectedly contact painful, distressing, or shaming scenes, including physical or sexual abuse, but that will occur only when the individual is ready to recover the scene, even if that has not been consciously decided ahead of time.

Toward an Integrated Self

Inner voices, self-nurturance, and *reparenting imagery* are vital tools which create security, promote integration of the self, and foster psychological health. Together they build a competent self. By owning our inner child, we regain a link with the past, with our own unique personal history. We need not remain prisoners of that history. We can cast away those old beliefs or attitudes which no longer suit us, thereby freeing us to live more consciously in the present. Letting go of the past together with living fully in the present are what make a different future possible.

CHAPTER 3

Conscious Management and Release of Affect

We learn to live consciously through becoming aware of inner and outer events *as they are happening*. Developing a conscious self means becoming increasingly aware of inner events, bodily events, and interpersonal events. A conscious self is able to experience in full awareness all of the distinctly different components of the self, including affects, needs, drives, and purposes. A conscious self lives consciously.

How do we create a conscious self? Let us come at this question from the direction of early language development. The inner life is initially experienced in a global, undifferentiated fashion out of which more distinguishable events emerge. Gradually, feelings differentiate from other inner events, say physiological drives, and also from one another. A central task of early language development is the *learning of names* for experienced events, whether external or internal. Unfortunately, many of us either learn the wrong labels or names for particular inner events or else we learn to hide those parts of the self which are not acceptable to significant others. For example, if a boy is consistently told he is excited whenever he expresses anger, he will learn to mislabel that primary feeling. Without the accurate name, the feeling itself will be denied to *conscious* awareness. When experiencing or expressing certain feelings is not acceptable, we learn to hide them, even from ourselves. If a young girl is consistently told, "Children aren't supposed to get angry at mother or father—that's bad," she may well lose awareness of her anger. In order to reverse this learning, we begin by learning how to *differentiate* and then *own* all of the components of the self. *Differen-*

tiated owning is the first key process which lies at the heart of living consciously, of creating a conscious self. Later we will consider *detachment, self-observation,* and *imagery.*

Differentiated Owning

Differentiated owning encompasses three crucial actions which promote conscious awareness within the self. First, owning means that a particular inner event, say, a feeling or need, is *experienced* consciously. Then it is recognized and *named* accurately. Finally, it is *owned* as an inherent part of the self. Owning is the pathway toward integration of the self.

Consider the following examples. If we feel irritation or hostility mounting inside, we first say to ourselves: "I feel angry." We name the feeling as anger and then own it, saying as it were, "I am angry and this is a natural part of me." Likewise, if we are either sad or anxious, we embrace these feelings consciously by naming them to ourselves and then owning them as inherent parts of our self. If we experience something quite different, a need to be alone, say, then we must behave similarly towards ourselves by first recognizing the need and naming it accurately. Finally, we consciously own the need as a vital part of us to be experienced, accepted, and embraced. More specific examples will follow our discussion of language.

The learning of names for inner events lies at the heart of differentiated owning. Language provides us with essential tools of mastery when confronting the inner life of the self. In conferring a name to a particular inner event, whether it be a feeling, need, or drive, the linguistic symbol provides a measure of self-understanding. It is from this vital knowledge of self, in which experienced events are named accurately, that conscious control in turn evolves. Clearly, language is central to the owning process, and, hence, to living consciously.

A LANGUAGE OF THE SELF

The task before us is creating a coherent image of the self as an evolving process which remains securely grounded in experience. We need an accurate language of the self which nevertheless keeps close to actual inner experience. The language to be presented is one that we have found most useful in promoting self-understanding and a competent self.

The image of the self presented here is an evolving integration derived from clinical observation, phenomenological experience, and the writing and observations of other investigators and theorists.[1]

These conceptions have further been observed developmentally and clinically in order to confirm both accuracy and usefulness in enhancing knowledge of self. The phenomenological experience of the self must be the test of our ideas, of the particular *language of the self* unfolding here.

People experience at least four primary motivational systems which together can be construed as interrelated parts of a unified self. These four are the *affect system, need system, drive system,* and *purpose system*. We will discuss each in turn in order to hone our language so that the words used to describe such inner states keep close to the ground of being.

AFFECT SYSTEM

We will begin with a consideration of the *affect system* because it has been fraught with confusion and widespread mislabeling. Dr. Silvan Tomkins has worked painstakingly toward developing a precise formulation of the primary affects or feelings. The affect system refers to the grouping of nine innate affects which Tomkins conceptualized. The following list summarizes Tomkins's formulation, in which the nine affects are distinguished, labeled as to both low and high intensity of experience, and described in terms of their respective facial responses:

Positive
1) Interest—Excitement: eyebrows down, track, look, listen
2) Enjoyment—Joy: smile, lips widened up and out

Resetting
3) Surprise—Startle: eyebrows up, eye blink

Negative
4) Distress—Anguish: cry, arched eyebrows, mouth down, tears, rhythmic sobbing
5) Fear—Terror: eyes frozen open, pale, cold, sweaty, facial trembling, with hair erect
6) Anger—Rage: frown, clenched jaw, red face

7) Shame—Humiliation: eyes down, head down
8) Dissmell: upper lip raised
9) Disgust: lower lip lowered and protruded

Any of the innate affects can be experienced singly or else in combination or sequence with other affects. For example, the most typically observed secondary reactions to shame are fear, distress (more commonly labeled sadness), and rage.[2]

Conscious access to the entire range of the innate affects is essential. Each feeling must be capable of expression by the self to the self. Expression of affects by the self to others, though important, is secondary to their being consciously experienced. The key is learning to recognize the internal signs of each affect and to name the affect accurately.

The point of our discussion is that names function like handles for our feelings. Knowing the accurate name allows us to handle the feeling, consider it consciously, then act upon it. When feelings are mis-named we remain caught in the net of affect; feelings can take us over or we fail to recognize a particular one. For example, anger is often denied access to awareness and it is also frequently confused with contempt which is a blend of anger and dissmell. Many individuals mistake the two. Anger protects us by keeping others away, whereas contempt elevates us above others. Contempt rejects whatever arouses that contempt. Anger and contempt feel different inwardly and to those toward whom our feelings are directed.

Shame has been another misunderstood affect. To feel shame is to feel *seen* in a painfully diminished sense. Whether all eyes are upon us or only our own, we feel deficient in some vital way as a human being. To live with shame is to feel never quite good enough to belong. In shame there is most intense self-consciousness, whereas in contempt there is least self-consciousness and most intense consciousness of the object which is experienced as permanently repudiated.

Affects are usually experienced in either rapid succession or complex combinations. When we are disappointed in our human relationships, our inner reactions typically comprise a mixture of such innate affects as shame, distress, rage, and fear. Specific affects become blended, creating our complex inner states, just as the primary colors become blended, creating something new. For example, blending shame and distress affects, and prolonging them over time, produces depression whereas blending shame and anger can produce jealousy. As already noted above, blending anger and dissmell produces contempt. These are all complex emotional states in contrast to the specific innate affects. Once we are able to distinguish and name these distinct feelings to ourselves, we discover essential tools of mastery. An accurate name directly provides us with knowledge of self and a measure of inner control.

Consider that universally experienced phenomenon, self-consciousness, for a moment. Many individuals experience binding self-consciousness when talking to strangers or at the prospect of public speaking. Self-consciousness is typically misunderstood as anxiety, the affect of fear. While anxiety may certainly *accompany* self-consciousness, they are not one and the same. Self-consciousness is a manifestation of shame, the feeling of exposure of the self. Our eyes turn inward in the midst of shame and we are suddenly watching ourselves in a painful, scrutinizing way, generating the torment of self-consciousness. Having the accurate name, furthermore, points out the direction of release. We will consider in depth how to release feelings when we explore the processes of detachment and self-observation.

Through having an accurate *language of the self* we are able to tune our feelings into conscious awareness. This produces knowledge of self, knowledge for action. Naming confers power.

NEED SYSTEM

Knowledge of and free access to our feelings are essential to psychological health. Equally essential is full awareness of the *need system*. The group of interpersonally based needs lies at the heart of human development. They are the foundations of human caring. The needs we experience in relation to other humans who become significant to us are the most vulnerable parts of the self.

Need for Relationship. Probably the most fundamental need of all is our need for relationship. Each of us experiences a need, from birth on, to be in relationship with one or more significant others. Each human partner experiences certain feelings, needs, and expectations in relation to the other. And each conveys a desire to enter the other's experiential world. Through reciprocal interest expressed over time, along with shared experiences of trust, a sense of security about the relationship gradually evolves. Such a condition of mutuality conveys to each participant that their relationship is real, honest, and mutually valued. It is through such a relationship that one feels genuinely understood, secure in the knowledge of being loved as a separate person in one's own right and wanted for oneself. Each comes to feel that their relationship truly is *wanted* by the other, in this way feeling special to the other.

Children need to experience such a distinct relationship with each parent in order to feel securely wanted by that parent. Both adolescents and adults continue to experience similar needs to be in relationship to other people with whom they can establish such lasting emotional ties, relinquish their strangeness, and thereby become significant to one another.

Far too frequently in this culture, individuals emerge into adulthood feeling such need for relationship either as too dangerous, likely to be disappointed, or else inherently shameful, a clear sign of deficiency. The cultural call to be independent and self-sufficient conflicts with the *needing* part of us. Countless individuals have assimilated the attitude that needing itself is shameful, a sign of inadequacy, as opposed to our view that needing is both natural and a source of strength.

Need for Touching, Holding. Adults as well as children experience needs for human touching or holding throughout life. Physical touching and holding is certainly one of our principal means of expressing tenderness or affection for one another. At certain times wanting to be held may be motivated by a need for bodily contact or bodily warmth per se. At other times, physical holding is a natural response to emotional need or distress. When emotional hurts motivate the need for physical comforting, holding communicates not so much affection as protection and security—the basis for trust.

Certainly daily expressions of affection through touching or hugging are vital in the course of living and, further, become means of replenishing our emotional stores. Such experiences of physical contact, whether by an arm around a shoulder or a hug, are certainly satisfying and pleasurable. There are still other moments when the self is feeling distraught, saddened, or otherwise in pain. These are the significant moments in our emotional lives which represent the *need for holding*.

Touching or holding, while certainly pleasurable, is *not* inherently sexual. There has been a widespread confusion of sexuality with physical holding in our culture and this has contributed to the sense of shame which so many individuals carry about this natural, universally experienced human need. Touching is pleasurable because it is a *sensory* experience. *Listening* to fine music, *seeing* a captivating movie, *tasting* a delicate meal, *smelling* fresh lilacs are all pleasurable experiences because these stimulate our sensory equipment. The skin is another of our sensory organs as Ashley Montagu has argued. Adequate sensory stimulation is required if infants are to mature in a healthy fashion. This is as true of touching as it is of the infant's other sensory organs. Our requirement for touching and holding does not suddenly cease as adolescence dawns; we never outgrow our vital, natural need for touching.

The cultural association of touching and sexuality is an emphatic one. Males in particular experience rather intense injunctions against touching one another. Peer group name-calling is one instrument by which the unfortunate association between the need for touching and sexuality is created. When our human needs to touch and hold one another become blocked or bound by shame, they will find either disguised or secret expression. Whether it is at the bar or on the gridiron, males find more culturally acceptable avenues to touch one another, albeit in a disguised manner. Even men and women will learn they must engage in sexual relations in order to simply hold one another in a fond embrace. When all voices in the culture tell us that the only reasons for wanting to feel especially close to another human being are sexual, eventually we will listen.

That is an unfortunate fact for we have in so doing denied ourselves the full range of what it means to be human. Certainly sexuality and the need for physical contact will shade into one another. However, touching which serves sexual ends must be distinguished from touching which expresses affection, and from holding which is needed to restore trust and security, to reaffirm one's own well-being.

Need for Identification. The need to identify is the wish to be like anyone deeply valued or admired, beginning in the family with parents and older siblings and extending to teachers in school, heroes, and eventually mentors. Observational learning through modeling is one vehicle through which identification occurs. Another is close and open communication between individuals, whether parent with child or mentor with novice, which then permits the one to feel essentially a part of the other. Phenomenologically, identification involves a merging with another, a partial giving up, even if only for a brief moment, of one's separate self. Sharing openly how we live and function *on the inside* as actual human beings enables others to join with us experientially through their own imagery and, in so doing, to *feel identified with* or a part of us. We identify in order to emulate those we admire, to feel *at-oneness* or belonging with these special ones and to enhance our sense of inner power by so doing. Experiences of identification become needed at critical times to provide support, strength, and healing for an evolving self.

Through having a network of significant others around us with whom we feel identified, we come to feel rooted and connected in a sense that is vital to people. In this manner identification further carries essential meaning as to where we belong.

Whenever we feel a need for direction or preparedness, having an external model available as a guide enables us to navigate situations that are uncertain or threatening. Learning how another has handled a particular situation enables us to feel prepared for it, whether or not we actually choose to follow that course. Through such close communication with a parent, mentor, or teacher in living, a sense of belonging grows.

Childhood and adolescence are times of preparation for adulthood. Preparedness and direction are especially urgent then but do not cease to be so. At each subsequent critical turn in development, such as marriage, parenthood, entering a trade, career or profession, or facing old age and death, we have a need for preparedness, for an external model which then can serve as an internal guide for the self.

Individuals will gravitate to one another throughout life in order to experience that kind of bonding implied in identification. In such a fashion, loyalties to groups evolve and begin to move us. We identify with a particular religion, a social cause, or a way of life and feel joined together. Perhaps it is a political party that wins our loyalty, or a football team. In either case we feel united in common purpose, we feel as one. And whether it is a racial group or a nation which sways us, loyalties can evolve into allegiances. The need to belong to someone or something, to feel identified with something larger than ourselves is dear to us. We yearn to feel a vital part of some group or cause or idea and thereby derive that precious sense of belonging somewhere.

Need for Differentiation. Every individual needs to differentiate his or her own unique self. This need is the instrument through which we individuate into distinctly separate and different selves. We feel a need to separate from those with whom we have identified. In this process, we sift the attitudes and practices acquired from others to discard those which either do not suit us or else have served their purpose and are no longer wanted. We allow those qualities, interests and talents which are most congruent with our essential self to emerge. To differentiate is to say, "This is me—I am different."

Differentiation and identification are fluctuating needs which alternate with one another throughout life. Each is central to the progress of the self in living.

The need to differentiate involves an internal push to separate from significant others, to become a separate self. Separation involves several developmental stages: separating first from mother, then establishing separate relationships with each parent, next separation from the family, and finally attaining a separate identity. Ultimately taking the reins of one's own life is central to building a secure, separate identity. In order to support these evolving separation efforts, competence building is necessary. The need to become a separate person does not occur in isolation but goes hand-in-hand with developing increasing mastery over one's own life. Individuals need to develop competence over things (leading ultimately to productive work) and competence with people (leading to satisfying human relationships) in order to feel secure enough to separate. The acquisition of mastery embraces both developing mastery over inner functioning and developing competence in the outer environment. The striving to differentiate is a striving to both separate and acquire mastery. Through these interwoven separation and mastery efforts we discover our own unique way of being a person.

Need to Nurture. We also experience needs to give to others, *to nurture* and put something back into the world. Whether it is affection we wish to verbalize or else a hug we wish to give, these are expressions of a basic human need. It may otherwise be felt as a desire to make or find some gift for someone regarded as special to us. There is nothing more primary than our need to express our caring and love for others, however it may be manifested. Our gift to another, whether it be time, assistance or caring, is *need*ful; it meets not only their need but our own as well.

There is an injunction in our culture not to be selfish, yet all our acts are precisely that: they are motivated by needs of our own. Even the most altruistic acts satisfy some inner need of the actor. The need to nurture others, which is the wellspring for altruism, is simply another of our most essential human needs.

Need for Affirmation. Each of us needs to feel that who we are, the inner person, is both worthwhile and valued. Through having someone significant provide that affirmation of self for us, gradually we learn how to give it to ourselves. We yearn to feel valued, recognized, singled out from the mass, seen as unique, different, and openly admired. This cry for recognition runs rampant through our experience. Society has not yet provided for the craving to feel worthy and valued in the world.

Those qualities by which we stand apart from others must be recognized and openly esteemed by significant others. Through having our own unique differences admired in this way, we begin to appreciate them in ourselves. The unique configuration of talents, interests and skills that evolves within us craves recognition by others so that we may feel truly valued as a self.

Need for Power. We began our exploration with the question: what is power? Let us reconsider what we have already examined. Our natural human need for power, to feel ourselves captains of our soul and destiny, is *not* inherently a need for power over others, but rather a need to feel in charge of our own lives. That is a human need of inestimable importance. Of course, the need may run amok, but it is most likely to do so as a result of early life experiences in which shame-humiliation and/or powerlessness have been either excessive or prolonged. It is then that power may become relied upon exclusively to either protect the self, compensate or reverse roles, culminating in a striving for power as a fundamental way of life. Power is a central human need which is not always interpersonally directed. It is as essential to the progress of the self in living as our primary needs for relationship, touching and holding, identification, differentiation, affirmation, and to nurture.

The need for power is closely related to the need for differentiation, although the phenomenological experience of the two is quite distinct. Differentiation is the instrument through which individuation comes about. To differentiate is to say: *I am different.* Differentiation involves an internal push to separate from significant others as well as a striving to acquire mastery which is aimed at supporting those separation efforts. Here is where the two needs begin to shade into one another. Gaining mastery over bodily functioning or psychic functioning and gaining competence over things or with people in the environment certainly enhance the inner sense of power as well as the need to differentiate, to declare oneself a unique self in one's own right. It is the *meaning* behind the mastery efforts which subtly distinguishes between the two needs. While this may seem like splitting hairs, the distinction is perhaps as subtle, and yet as essential, as the distinction between touching which serves sexual ends and touching which expresses affection or holding which is needed to restore trust and security.

Power is a vital human need which must be recognized, acknowledged and responded to positively by parents, by teachers, and especially by ourselves. We must learn how to build power into our lives as well as maintain power in relation to others. We must also learn how to take back the power in numerous situations encountered in the natural course of living in which we are rendered powerless.

Power itself is the fulcrum upon which hope and despair delicately balance. When we are rendered powerless in any significant area of our lives, we are most susceptible to depression, hopelessness and eventually, utter despair. Death of a spouse or significant other, loss of a job or major life role, or loss of a bodily function or sound health are each a profound threat to security and potentially render us acutely powerless. Powerlessness itself is a regressive experience which, if prolonged, threatens our ability to sustain courage and hope. Helplessness and hopelessness are a dangerous combination, as Viktor Frankl observed forty years ago in a concentration camp: "Those who know how close the connection is between the state of mind of a man—his courage and hope, or lack of them—and the state of immunity of his body will understand that the sudden loss of hope and courage can have a deadly effect."[3] Dr. O. Carl Simonton reports a parallel observation in connection with recent cancer research.[4] Feelings of hopelessness, helplessness, depression, and despair have been reported to precede cancer, leading Simonton to theorize about the suppressive effect of such emotional responses to stress upon the body's immune system as one contributing factor in the onset of cancer.

The wellspring of power is the long childhood of helplessness into

which we are thrust at birth and from which we ever so gradually
emerge. It is that enduring experience, itself shrinking through maturation, which conditions our need for power, yet to which we are
inevitably thrust back by subsequent events that threaten our essential control over our own lives.

DRIVE SYSTEM

The *need system* is a second primary, motivational subsystem
within the self, additional to the *affect system*. The third major
component of the self is the *drive system:* biological requirements
such as hunger, thirst, sex, sleep, oxygen, and relief from pain. Of all
the physiological drives the one given especial prominence has been
the sexual drive. While there are certainly both learned and social
components to human sexuality, there remains a biological sub-
stratum which has come to be known as the sexual drive. Sexuality
manifests initially through exploratory genital touching, mastur-
batory activities, childhood sexual play, and sexual curiosity. When
puberty is unleashed, genital sexuality emerges with vigor through
various adolescent sexual strivings. Later adult sexual expression,
integrated within the self, completes the picture.

The physiological drives do not remain isolated but become significantly fused with affects, as Silvan Tomkins has demonstrated.[5]
This is true of sexuality and it is equally true for the hunger drive.
Each drive can become associated and fused with the affects of
either excitement and enjoyment or else shame and disgust.[6] For
example, the excitement affect in sexual excitement is no different
than excitement affect about any other activity under the heavens,
according to Tomkins. There is a distinct fusion of affect and drive in
sexuality; sexuality indeed *requires* amplification by excitement affect for potency. However, excitement does *not* require amplification
by sexuality in order to seize the individual. The primacy of the
affects over drives is further confirmed by the analogous fusion of
sexuality with the affects of shame or contempt. Instead of producing
potency, this latter fusion will lead to the disruption of sexuality
through sexual blocks or the actual disowning of sexuality. Thus,
sexual potency requires a fusion of the sexual drive with the positive
affects of excitement and enjoyment.

Experiencing sexuality with enjoyment or excitement creates pleasure, a positive experience for the self. When a young boy is ob-

served to be masturbating and is told, "I know that feels good but we do that in private," sexuality remains associated with positive affects while accepted social convention is transmitted. Alternatively, a response such as, "Don't touch yourself *there,* that's disgusting," will begin the association of sexuality with shame and/or contempt. Following sufficient shaming responses, sexual expression itself may become bound by shame. Sex will then spontaneously activate either shame or self-contempt. Fusion with positive affect will result in eventual integration of the sexual drive as a natural part of the self while fusion with shame or disgust will lead to the disowning of sexuality.

In addition to the direct effects of affect-drive fusion, experiences with a drive itself or through relationship to others become translated into words. We link those words together over time, creating meanings about the self. Failure to measure up to any particular cultural standard of sexual performance or attractiveness unfortunately may create feelings of inner deficiency, shame. Feelings of specific inadequacy can spread throughout the self so that a woman who believes herself less sexually responsive than some imagined norm may come to experience herself as a failure. Hence, physiological drives become overlaid with essential meaning as to our inherent worth or adequacy as men and women.

PURPOSE SYSTEM

The fourth central component in our unfolding language of the self is the *purpose system,* the demands and pressures experienced from within which represent basic definitions of "who we are" and "what we want to become." These definitions of self reflect our core purposes in living, our dreams for ourselves and basic expectations from life's many pursuits, including career, marriage, and family.

People live within the context of personal history, stretching from past memories through the present moment into an unknown future to which we are drawn or called. We carry forward vital goals, hopes, and visions to which we aspire. Through our imagination we sense what is dimly seen ahead for us; imagination engages us in our future. Through our inner vision we inherit our destiny to become shapers of the landscape, no longer merely figures in it.

Purposes are those compelling dreams we have for ourselves which pull us through life, the central goals for which we live.

Though in different language, both Alfred Adler and Viktor Frankl have pointed to the vitality of future goals as motivators. Through having an essential dream in life we feel a sense of purpose to our lives. We feel useful, our lives now matter. Something off in the future awaits us and we live guided by that dream, that vision of purpose, propelled toward it. The goals we live for embrace a set of dreams which gives life personal meaning, purpose.

Future scenes of purpose are not static but changing. As development unfolds we experience recurring crises of self-definition. Let us consider for a moment who we were, who we are now, and where we are going in life. Think back to the time when you were ten years old. Do you remember who you were back then, what kind of person you were on the threshold of life's unfolding? What dreams did you have for yourself?

Now move forward ten years and recapture what living meant at age twenty. What did you want most out of life at this point? What mattered most in living?

Let us move ahead to age thirty. Who were you then, what kind of person? What were your goals, your hopes and dreams for yourself at that juncture?

Now consider the present moment: what are you living for *now?* Do you feel that basic satisfaction with self that comes from living well? And if not, where do you look for that validation? What are the reasons for the life you lead and the work you do? What do you get out of it and what are the costs to you personally? Is there anything else in life you would either rather be doing or else also like to experience before death takes you?

And finally, what of the *future:* what do you want most out of life in the years ahead? What truly matters most in this next portion of life?

These are difficult, even frightening questions we must ask ourselves at various points throughout life. Periodically, we need to consciously review our lives in order to know if we are living up to our basic expectations of ourselves.

Life is a process in which periods of stability, certainty, and direction alternate with periods of confusion, uncertainty, and inner searching. The periods of questioning and searching are what eventually give birth to clarity. We arrive at new goals for living or else at new reasons for continuing in the same pursuits. Now these new goals or reasons carry us only for a period of time, not forever.

Then a time comes when they carry us no longer and we embark once again upon that inner searching for direction. We begin to ask ourselves: What do I want out of life *now?* What do I want to do with my life *now?* In essence, what are the *goals* I am living for? It is as if we have become restless once more and struggle to resolve our discontent. In response to this, we feel a need to change something in our lives.

Love relationships and vocation are two principal commitments that we make in life. We experience these alternating periods of stability/instability in relation to each of these primary commitments. The reasons we enter a vocation or a marriage carry us for, say, five to seven years. Then we may find ourselves questioning, again feeling discontent either with our work or with our marriage. It makes sense that the people who enter a marriage will grow and change over time, or else the reasons they originally got married are no longer true about them. As their individual growth unfolds, their relationship must change as well to suit their evolving needs. The reasons we enter a particular vocation will likewise change over a period of years. We are no longer quite the same individual or else the challenge has gone out of it. Once again we find ourselves questioning our aims or direction.

The periods of certainty and stability last approximately five to seven years before the next phase of inner discontent and searching sets in. Then, with regard to vocation or relationships, either we find new reasons to stay in it, or we change it somehow, or else we leave it. These developmental cycles are recurring crises of purpose through which identity evolves.

To be a self is to have a system of guiding dreams, a place inside where we *locate* the self we are: that final place from which we will not be moved. What offends our inner self, we cannot abide. Through our most cherished dreams in living we know the self we are. Dreams give us something to die for. If there is nothing to die for, what is there to live for? Dreams touch the epistemological/spiritual ground of being. They give meaning and direction to our lives: we feel useful, our lives matter, we experience purpose.

There is presently in our culture a growing crisis of purpose. We lack something to believe in with conviction. There is a spiritual void in the midst of our materialistic-technological society. We have lost our spiritual identity wherein is imbedded our quest for meaning. We are giants without souls.

Having an aim in life, a goal to live for, is as vital today for the unemployed worker, a person with cancer, or an individual bereft of spouse as it was for the concentration camp prisoner, according to Viktor Frankl. Purposes are imbedded in the natural developmental flow of human life and resurface with renewed force in the face of life events which threaten anything of significance to us. If we give way to despair, and lose faith in the future, in *our* future, we are doomed. We must retain a hold on ourselves by having an aim in life, a purpose to live for. These aims and purposes are the essential dreams we hold most dear.

THE SELF AS AN EVOLVING PROCESS

We have articulated an image of the self embracing four motivational systems, the *affect, need, drive,* and *purpose* systems. These are interrelated yet distinguishable components of the self in action. Together they provide us with an accurate *language of the self* which remains grounded in inner experience. Through having *names* for the group of innate affects, the group of primary needs, the primary drives, and purposes, we now have vital tools for creating a truly conscious self.

We need to be able to experience consciously all of these different yet interrelated parts of a unified self. We must be able to distinguish one feeling from another if we are to know when we are angry as opposed to either ashamed or afraid. Likewise, we must be able to say to ourselves, "I need to be with a friend," as opposed to "I need to be alone right now."

When we can consciously experience and accurately name our feelings, needs, drives, and purposes, then we are enabled to feel a sense of inner mastery. In addition, the sooner we become aware of our feelings, the more able we are to experience a measure of conscious choice, say, over just how sad we feel or how afraid we become. Hence, *naming* is integral to living competently, to acquiring a fuller measure of inner conscious control.

Following the naming of feelings, needs, etc., comes *owning* each as an inherent part of the self. All feelings are valid. They are not to be questioned, criticized, or judged. Feelings are not good or bad, they just *are*. Likewise, all of our human needs are valid and must be experienced, named, and finally owned as natural parts of the self.

Evolving an accurate language of the self is essential. Conscious awareness and inner choice enhance our sense of inner power, producing self-esteem and psychological health.

CONSULTATION WITH SELF

Feelings, needs, drives, and purposes must be consciously consulted and then owned as an inherent part of the self. The process of making inner events conscious, owning and finally integrating them, must be engaged in rather consistently. Parts of the self that have been blocked from experience, such as the feeling of shame or anger, the need to touch or hold or be held, our needs for belonging or for separating, or our sexuality, can be recontacted and re-owned through consistent conscious effort. Often the inner blocks we experience are created by shame, contempt, or fear. Through consciously working with ourselves to free the part of the self blocked or disowned, we are gradually enabled to recontact it experientially. Once we remember to keep it conscious we can begin the learning of names. We give that part of the self a name that both fits our experience and allows us to *handle it,* as it were. To back up our awareness of a feeling or need blocked from conscious awareness, we look for the signs which tell us of its presence and we work to make conscious the feeling or need itself. Likewise with the sex drive. And then we embrace it, saying within, "This is a natural, vital part of me."

There is a tool which translates this owning process into action: *consultation with self.* If something were dropped at the other end of the room you are now sitting in, your attention would immediately shift to it. Imagine the focus of attention as a spotlight which we can direct, both point and aim. When we consciously consult ourselves, we deliberately and actively focus attention inwards to make inner events more distinct. We tune in to ourselves, to our *feelings: How am I feeling today? If I'm sad or angry, how come? What is the source of my feeling and what can I do about it?* Then we tune in to our *needs* and listen inside: *Am I needing anything right now and, if so, what?* We listen next to our bodies, to how rested we feel or warm or hungry. These are physiological states or drives which require periodic attention. *Drives* such as sex can be made more natural by consciously tuning in to them on a consistent daily basis: *Am I feeling sexual?* And finally with regard to *purposes,* those precious goals for which we live, we similarly consult ourselves in order to know them: *What do I want most out of life? What matters most to me in living? What are my dreams?* Through consulting ourselves we make each of these different parts of the self both conscious and a living part of us. We allow ourselves literally to *have the experience.*

Let us consider how this tool has been utilized and practiced by participants in the course. Maureen told us: "The *consulting self* tool was the most revealing and has become an indispensable method for understanding my needs and responding to them. I put myself *first* sometimes now because I can acknowledge my needs. My days are hectic and many people make demands, my work is never done and this hasn't changed; but now I let my needs receive attention during the day, not just after 5:00 p.m." Carol followed with her reflections: "I used this tool to find out how my body was feeling and what I was needing at particular moments. Often I was able to catch myself in a mood that could've developed into deeper anxiety or depression, had I not thought about things and made better choices as to how I responded to my inner feelings. Usually a deliberate change in thinking or behavior followed which would put me in a better mood. I learned to get into myself to find out what was really going on inside of me, why it was and how I could change it." Jim added his thoughts: "Consulting myself has been useful because I used to ignore any stressful signs or pain, but now I can deal with situations better because I find out how I feel about everything."

Learning to take time out of our busy schedules and listen inwardly is a valuable tool for living more consciously inside ourselves. It can lead to changed behavior in relation to others as well as oneself. Consider Jean's reactions to the tool: "I know I need to spend more time doing this because it's a totally new experience for me. Now I will consult myself and so not have to agree with every single thing that is said in a conversation. In the past I've been a chameleon, not that I wanted to, but I didn't see how to not be." Sarah added: "The biggest thing I've learned is the importance of confronting and identifying my own feelings. I do this by listening to my body's needs and changing my behavior to determine what satisfies my needs." Jennifer chimed in: "This one is particularly useful in times of crisis. When I am angry or depressed, this tool is one which lets me label what I'm feeling and attack it. I use it in conjunction with the happiness-adequacy lists." Rudy spoke up: "Rather than drifting, I am more aware of what direction I need and want to take. This tool has helped me to stop and consider what I want to do. Listening to my body has helped me to slow down and pay more attention to stress reactions." Steve agreed, saying: "I really like this. It's a quick way to get a focus on what's happening inside. I use it almost every day. It's very useful for thinking back and isolating the 'triggers' that precede my worst feelings of anger, disappointment, or shame." Each of these individuals has experienced living more consciously, more securely guided from within. Awareness of their inner life has become enlarged, thereby enhancing competence.

As a final example of the tool in action, consider Jeff, who when he turned thirty-five, found himself in the grip of a mid-life crisis. Unexpectedly, that profound inner questioning once more erupted. Since he had lived out thirty-five years, life had essentially reached its midpoint. He realized he did not have all the time in the world left to accomplish his goals. The afternoon of life was passing quietly. He suddenly found himself asking: What do I want most out of life in the next thirty-five years? Jeff's mid-life transition had arrived and was in essence a crisis of purpose. He wanted to live this next portion of life as consciously as he was able, in keeping with his inner self, his own needs and dreams for himself.

The inner searching Jeff embarked upon preoccupied him for well over one full year and involved an active discovery of purpose: What mattered most in life for him? What did he truly value in living? What dreams did he have for himself? Knowing that life was not forever, what mattered most in the years ahead? These were the central questions he concerned himself with over the ensuing months.

Then the questioning began to spread out. He found himself asking a question he never dreamed to ask: Do I even want to remain a college professor or is there any other pursuit I would rather follow? That was a frightening thing to ask, for how often do we retreat from the cutting edge of living out of fear of asking life's deepest questions?

Jeff proceeded to use *consulting self* on a daily basis in order to make his dreams fully conscious and he seriously considered many other possible vocations. He imagined himself working at different occupations which had interested him, from woodworking and ceramics to managing a restaurant. Jeff imagined waking up in the morning living somewhere else and going to work at a new occupation, in this way living out a different vocation through visual imagery. He made the imagery as realistic and vivid as possible to know how well the particular choice suited him.

The most important discovery Jeff made was that he *did* want to remain a college professor. His work meant a great deal to him, but he sensed himself moving in new directions. Through consulting self, Jeff learned the value and meaning of what he was already doing and so felt he could continue in his profession with a renewed sense of purpose.

As these examples illustrate, individuals can be taught how to focus attention inwards in order to listen to and make conscious such inner events as feelings and needs. Likewise, learning to listen to one's body becomes a valuable tool for monitoring bodily stress reactions. Increased effectiveness in living is the fruit of such labors.

Through actively consulting each of our four motivational systems, we promote their integration within the self in full conscious awareness. By consulting ourselves, we learn to own, to embrace, and to claim all of the distinctly different parts of us. The owning process is a vital tool which develops a conscious self.

Detachment

The ability to experience, name, and own those distinguishable parts of the self is a necessary developmental task which can be learned. It is certainly central to living consciously as we have just seen. But if that were all we could do with inner states, we would remain partially caught in the net of happenstance. We must attain a fuller measure of conscious control over our inner lives to live from a position of power, from a truly conscious *center*. Evolving an accurate language of the self promotes conscious awareness and, eventually, re-integration of those differentiated parts within the self. The owning process lies at the heart of conscious integration of the self, but requires a second process to complete it.

Being capable of experiencing feelings, as well as the other parts of the self, is important to growth. Yet we are apt to be swept away in the onrushing flood of affect unless we are able to detach from, or let go of, particularly intense feelings which have been aroused.

The process of *detachment* is a second wellspring of living consciously. The essence of detachment is learning to step back from a particular feeling or situation in order to *observe* it consciously and then let go of it. The key is learning to hold a part of the self back as a "friendly observer" of both inner and outer events. Observing consciously means being neither critical nor judgmental but, rather, *fully conscious in the present moment*.

There are inevitable occasions when we become so *identified* with a particular feeling like anger that it takes us over. We *become* the feeling and lose both perspective and our center. If we can step back enough to observe the feeling or situation, we immediately begin to let go of it and regain our center. The feeling then will pass.

Consider the following comments from Irene, a participant in the course: "I have learned how to detach myself from a situation, especially when dealing with jealousy. If I can look at the situation as though I'm not a part of it, many times I see how irrational I'm being." Viktor Frankl described the process of detachment under extreme circumstances, the concentration camp:

"I remember a personal experience. Almost in tears from pain (I had terrible sores on my feet from wearing torn shoes), I limped a few kilometers with our long column of men from the camp to our work site. Very cold, bitter winds struck us. I kept thinking of the endless little problems of our miserable life. What would there be to eat tonight? If a piece of sausage came as extra ration, should I exchange it for a piece of bread? Should I trade my last cigarette, which was left from a bonus I received a fortnight ago, for a bowl of soup? How could I get a piece of wire to replace the fragment which served as one of my shoelaces? Would I get to our work site in time to join my usual working party or would I have to join another, which might have a brutal foreman? What could I do to get on good terms with the Capo, who could help me to obtain work in camp instead of undertaking this horribly long daily march?

"I became disgusted with the state of affairs which compelled me, daily and hourly, to think of only such trivial things. I forced my thoughts to turn to another subject. Suddenly I saw myself standing on the platform of a well-lit, warm and pleasant lecture room. In front of me sat an attentive audience on comfortable upholstered seats. I was giving a lecture on the psychology of the concentration camp! All that oppressed me at that moment became objective, seen and described from the remote viewpoint of science. By this method I succeeded somehow in rising above the situation, above the sufferings of the moment, and I observed them as if they were already of the past. Both I and my troubles became the object of an interesting psychoscientific study undertaken by myself."[7]

Usually we find little need to let go of joyous events. We feel them however intensely and even find joy rekindled through sharing it with others. Affect is indeed contagious. Positive affects give us little cause to detach, yet we invariably find that we tend to let go of good feelings too easily. We must learn to let go of negative situations and negative feelings such as anger, shame, and fear. We must learn to let go of the past, especially our mistakes and failings.

Developing a capacity for detachment is one of the most challenging tasks of inner development. Fortunately, a variety of tools for accomplishing detachment are available to us. We will consider four different ones: humor, detachment imagery, refocusing attention, and meditation.

HUMOR

Being able to find something humorous about a situation enables us to step outside of it enough to detach from it. Whenever we can respectfully laugh about ourselves or some situation we find ourselves in, perspective is immediately restored. Humor allows us to step outside of the situation just enough so that we can observe it. Once we have done so, we have already detached and are then more able to let go of it. This was one of the tools Viktor Frankl utilized as a way of coping with being in the concentration camp. He and another prisoner made a pact to make up one amusing story from the day's events to tell each other at night. Being capable of seeing the humor in a situation, however distasteful or inhuman it may be, is a vital survival skill.

One man we know who was accident-prone in a small way used to harass himself for breaking or dropping things. Through the course he learned how to find something humorous about his mishaps and would frequently comment aloud in order to help himself detach. For example, when he spilled a cup of coffee he would say, "Gravity strikes again!"

DETACHMENT IMAGERY

Letting go of those negative feelings which otherwise might continue to spiral within us requires learning an *inner discipline*. We must learn to become strict as well as tender with ourselves as we might with a wayward child. For example, when you leave your office at the end of the day, try to be strict with yourself: consciously leave behind all of the day's accumulated tensions, worries, and pressures. They will all be there in the morning to greet you again.

Imagine putting them all in a desk drawer. Then consciously take home with you only the good feelings, the small successes and accomplishments of the day. In effect, you are using imagery to create an imaginary container for troublesome feelings.

Detachment is a very conscious process requiring both discipline and strictness. There is another way in which detachment imagery can be utilized, namely, in handling matters involving doubt or conflict which do not require an immediate decision. If we allowed our conscious self to be continually preoccupied by doubt or worry, we would become immobilized. A device we can employ is to imagine a "stove top" inside with six or eight burners. Upon each sits a covered pot. When confronted with an issue or conflict requiring conscious reflection, we can take it out for conscious examination through *consulting self*. After a period of reflection, we consciously put the problem in one of our *back pots* and then imagine placing the cover on it. This frees our conscious self from being preoccupied with the matter in question. At a later time we again take it out for *consultation with self* and again return it. Concerns which are not immediate or are beyond our control are best handled in this two-fold manner.

There are occasions in the course of life which present us with choices about which we feel strong, opposing sets of feelings. It is useful when we are feeling *ambivalent* to periodically take the matter out for conscious review. Through *consulting self* we take a conscious reading on it. Then we put it away in a back pot until the next period of conscious considering. In this manner we can observe which way we feel about the issue on each occasion of consultation with ourselves. We can watch to see if our response to the choice at hand is rather consistent, either consistently positive or negative, or else mixed. Consulting self together with detachment imagery provide us with a set of tools useful for decision-making.

REFOCUSING ATTENTION

The process of detachment involves an effortful shifting of the focus of attention. This allows us to step back from or outside of a particular feeling or situation in order to observe it consciously and ultimately let go of it. Instead of focusing attention *inwards* in order to *experience* inner events, as in consulting self, we are now refocusing attention *elsewhere* in order to *observe* them. Many feelings can spiral when activated: anxiety into panic; anger into rage; and shame into humiliation, inferiority, and worthlessness. These are occasions

when it is necessary to refocus attention *outside* ourselves rather
than inside.

When feelings are spiraling within us, there are several useful tools
available for refocusing attention in the necessary manner which
then accomplishes *letting go*. Refocusing attention back outside
ourselves can be accomplished, for example, by becoming immersed
in physical activities like jogging, swimming, and bicycling. By
focusing attention upon the activity itself, we refocus attention *outside* ourselves, enabling us to let go within. It is this refocusing of
attention which permits us to experience a measure of inner detachment. By letting go we release worries or concerns and both relax
and quiet the self.

Another way of accomplishing this form of detaching is through
becoming immersed in any external sensory experience, particularly
one that is both visual and physical. For example, going outside for a
walk, then seeing and listening to the sights and sounds of the world,
will refocus attention outwardly. Even talking to oneself about what
one sees and hears will enable the self to detach from whatever
negative feelings might be spiraling.

A related example comes to mind. One woman we know cleans
closets whenever she gets depressed. These activities refocus attention back outside herself and enable her gradually to detach from the
depression. And at least she can feel productive.

Let us consider other examples which illustrate how particular
individuals in the course have put this tool, refocusing attention, to
work for themselves. Cathy was first: "I do this best at work when I
refocus my attention on customers who need help. When someone
else wants attention, I have a better reason to use the tool. And when
I'm not at work, I pretend to do this with other people, I mean
refocus attention on other people, without actually doing anything
but imagining it." Jim joined in: "I don't do this regularly, except
through activities like swimming. I do it often in the sense that when
I identify something bothering me, I evaluate its worth and if it's
minimal, as it often is, then I just tell myself it's not worth worrying
about." Refocusing attention is a tool for letting go of negative
feelings, mistakes, and failings. Attention can be refocused either
onto a physical task of some kind or else directly into external
sensory experience. The key is consciously refocusing attention
outside ourselves.

Diane's experience was illustrative: "I learned this some years ago when I took out one of the kid's bicycles during a moment of absolute frustration. After pumping up and down hills, I returned home feeling great. Now I have my own bike." Others had considerable difficulty mastering this tool in spite of realizing its value. Jean reported the following: "I swim, knit, talk with friends. But most often I just become depressed. The inability to 'let go' is probably my single most serious problem. I hold grudges against everyone, including (especially) myself. Unfortunately, I hold grudges often and let bad feelings dominate me." Sarah was more hopeful: "I tend to let my feelings spiral a lot, as I've noticed. This tool has helped me a great deal in pinpointing the problem and helping me to handle it."

Detachment never comes quickly or easily but requires consistent conscious practice, often over months to a year, to attain. But it is learnable. The key is determination along with experimenting to find the particular tools which suit each unique person. There is no *one* right way of utilizing the tool.

Learning how to refocus attention in this manner is especially useful in reversing the effects of shame. The affect termed shame can be experienced in the form of *embarrassment, self-consciousness,* or *shyness.*

The following passage illustrates the application of this tool to overcoming shyness:

> "Many of us experience shyness when faced with the prospect of approaching a stranger. The immediate feeling may be one of either self-consciousness or embarrassment. We may stammer inside, not knowing quite what to say. We may even feel altogether speechless and urgently seek a way to escape or hide, though a part of us secretly longs to reach out directly to that other person. Yet we feel too self-conscious to move even on the urge and, feeling bound-up, now feel trapped. In response to that inner conflict, we hang our head, avert our eyes, and let the moment slip away.
>
> "Contained in the experience of shyness is the feeling of shame, of exposure of oneself. It is this feeling of exposure which characterizes the essential nature of shame. To feel shame is to be seen. Our eyes suddenly turn inward and our attention unexpectedly focuses wholly upon ourselves. Suddenly, we are watching ourselves, scrutinizing the minutest detail of our being. This excruciating observation of the self generates the torment of self-consciousness which in turn creates that binding and paralyzing effect upon the self.
>
> "Shyness is to be understood . . . as shame either in the presence of

or at approaching strangers. The presence of the stranger sets off the feeling of exposure which results in what many of us have come to call shyness. What *really* is being thus exposed you might wonder? Imagine ignoring one's impulse to turn away. Imagine going ahead in spite of feeling shy and actually approaching that stranger: *What would I say? I'd look foolish, stupid, clumsy even. I wouldn't know what to do. I'd die inside.* It is the very self inside of us which feels exposed in shame.

"Before moving on let's consider the implications of such a view for how best to grow beyond the barrier shame sets us in the form of shyness. This will highlight the developmental relevance of the particular conception of shame unfolding here. First of all we must give ourselves learning time, time to make mistakes as we go about the task of learning something new. And learning how to approach strangers is a skill that can be learned if we are willing to practice. Permission to fail is part of it. Permission to look foolish, even dumb, both to ourselves and to those others as well.

"Then we must *practice,* practice going up to strangers and *expect* to fail some of the time. Expect that it won't work out and let failing be okay. We must learn to be gentle with ourselves. We must learn to treat ourselves kindly and lovingly and with forgiveness for our most imperfect humanness. It doesn't have to work out each time or necessarily even most of the time. And it's okay if we blow it all the time. It's also okay to be just plain shy. Only when *however we are* becomes good enough do we ever become really free to be our best.

"Next, we must learn how to reverse that internal shame process. When our eyes become focused internally upon ourselves, we must learn to exert real conscious effort to focus all of our attention once again back outside. Becoming visually and/or physically involved in the world is one way of accomplishing that reversal. An example of this would be to become absorbed in the sights and sounds of the world around us. Focusing upon any such sensory experience, whether visual or physical, can enable the self to accomplish that much-needed refocusing of attention. Even talking to oneself about the things one sees or hears or touches can aid the self in letting go of shame. If we are able to refocus our attention once more outside ourselves, the feeling of exposure, of shame, itself will pass. And in this way we are able to gain increasing control over the binding effects shame is able to have upon us.

"Another way of accomplishing this necessary refocusing of attention is by observing just what kind of person this stranger is *instead of* worrying about what the stranger thinks of us. When we are considering how *we* feel about another, whether it is someone we like, respect or might want to get to know, we are in a position of *equal power* in relation to the other. On the other hand, when our attention is instead focused entirely upon ourselves, upon how well or badly we are coming off or how the other sizes us up, this inner stance leaves us feeling rather *powerless* and hence more vulnerable to shame. With sufficient practice and determination we can learn how to switch from a relatively powerless position to one of more equal power in relation to others.

"Each time we can reverse the process, each time we can go ahead and approach a stranger, however well or badly it goes, we gain increasing freedom to do it again and again and again. For the feeling of exposure begins to lose some of the paralyzing hold it has had upon us. And strangers are no longer as apt to trigger that binding feeling in the first place.

"Of course, there will always be times when shyness recurs, times when we are once again vulnerable to shame. That is to be expected throughout life. And those are times when we ought to be tender with ourselves, neither critical nor punitive.

"In these ways, we can learn to better tolerate shame in whatever form, shyness being one, and to be much less fearful of its recurrence. For we have also learned how best to cope with it when it does come upon us and, most especially, how to let go of that binding feeling of exposure.[8]

MEDITATION

Refocusing attention is one critical tool for developing the capacity for detachment. Another important tool is meditation which is, in essence, a one-point focusing of attention. There are many schools of meditation which teach different forms of this particular inner discipline. Attention is focused on one point, such as a repeated sound, one's breathing itself, an object to be contemplated, or breath counting.

Then one allows all feelings, thoughts, memories, images, or fantasies simply to come into awareness and then to pass through awareness. The task is to *observe* the contents of consciousness by focusing all attention on one point. In this manner, the process of letting go is accomplished. Meditation is a way of quieting the self that teaches us another means to develop inner detachment.[9]

Individuals prone to recurring fears or worries may find the "Bubble Meditation" particularly useful for learning to detach or let go. One woman who was plagued by fears of crashing whenever she boarded an airplane, learned to place each recurring worry inside its bubble and then watch it float away. In this way she gradually was able to manage her fear through detaching from it.

We have rounded out our discussion of detachment with a consideration of meditation as another useful tool in promoting the capacity to live more consciously. Meditation, refocusing attention, detachment imagery, and humor are each unique translations of the principle of detachment into living action. Each is an activity which the self consciously engages in to release the hold of powerful affects such as anger, fear, or shame. Through learning how to let go of feelings, we live more securely grounded within ourselves and reap a harvest of inner power. Whenever we are able to take essential charge over ourselves, including both our reactions and attitudes, we remain centered in a position of power within, even when the outward situation is a powerless one. Learning how to detach either from inner feelings or situations beyond our control is a skill, an essential developmental task, which reduces shame and directly enhances personal power and self-esteem.

Self-Observation:
Directing the Focus of Attention

We have now considered two radically different processes which complement one another. Differentiated owning involves a conscious focusing of attention *inwards* whereas detachment involves a conscious *stepping back* from a feeling in order to observe it and let go of it. Consciously refocusing attention outwards is only one technique for accomplishing detachment. Let us review this once more. Think of the focus of attention as a spotlight which we can direct. We can focus attention inwards in order to listen for and experience such inner events as feelings or needs. We likewise can listen to our bodies' states and drives. Alternatively, we can focus attention outside ourselves into external sensory experiences such as going for a walk or immersing oneself in music. Attention also can be focused onto a physical task whether it be jogging, swimming, or cleaning closets. And finally, attention can be focused on one point as in many methods of meditation.

Each of these processes carries an additional element of *observation*. When we consult ourselves about, say, how we are feeling at a particular moment, a part of us is searching to *experience* what is present while another part *observes* upon that experience in order to name it, own it, etc. Likewise, in refocusing attention or in meditation, a part of the self is directly experiencing events while another part detaches from that experience in order to *observe* either outwardly or else the experience itself.

Whenever we are able to observe upon our experience, we immediately detach from it. *Self-observation*[10] is critical to developing the capacity for detachment and is entirely different from binding self-consciousness as described earlier. The torment of self-consciousness is a manifestation of shame, the feeling of *exposure* of the self. Self-observation, on the other hand, is of a completely different nature; it neither binds nor torments. Nor is it a splitting of the self into parts that are owned and parts that are disowned. Quite the contrary, for self-observation involves learning to hold a part of the self back inside as a *friendly observer*. This enables us to experience events fully while *simultaneously* observing upon our experience. When we are able both to experience and simultaneously observe our experience, we become fully conscious in the moment.

Learning to hold a part of the self back as a friendly observer means actively detaching that part of the self within, which then can *observe* the remaining parts of the self as well as outer events. When a part of the self is able to remain detached and observing, we stay centered as well as conscious in any interpersonal situation even while we are yet in it. Through detaching a part of the self to remain an observer, we ultimately build a *conscious center* which we are neither born with nor come upon automatically. Having a conscious center, a part of the self which remains detached and observes, integrates all of the many different parts within the self such as affects, needs, and drives. Developing a conscious, integrated self is facilitated through learning how to *divide attention* by simultaneously observing upon one's experience. Why is this useful? Because it is through creating such a conscious self that we gain essential competence in living.

Consider a young man, Alex, who struggles with doubts and insecurities for much of his life. He questioned his very worth or adequacy either in particular relationships or else in valued pursuits such as career. The fact that someone cared about him yesterday was no assurance that he or she would feel similarly today. The doubts recurred and once again, Alex put his basic worth or lovableness up for grabs, as it were. Teaching well on one occasion allowed him to feel a measure of adequacy for that moment only. On the next occasion, Alex would again put his adequacy on the line, either to be confirmed or disconfirmed. He had not learned how to remain feeling worthy and adequate beyond question.

When these doubts of his recurred, he over-identified with them. Alex located his own self not among his strengths and competencies, of which there were many, but directly within the doubts which plagued him. By identifying with them, not only did he more soundly believe them, but even more importantly, he *became* them.

Since it was he who put his adequacy or worth up for grabs in the first place, Alex first had to learn how not to do so. That was his initial task: actively learning how to keep his inner sense of worth and adequacy separate from life's vicissitudes, disconnected from whatever happened to him out in the world. When doubts, insecurities or worries returned, Alex had to learn not to identify with them, but rather to stay detached by observing them consciously.

Through holding part of the self back inside, we create a "friendly observer" which remains outside of disturbing inner events or feeling states. Whenever Alex was able, however briefly, to actually observe his doubts rather than become entirely identified with them, he remained more secure within. His essential self was then located not among those doubts but directly within that inner friendly observer.

Learning to detach a part of the self and hold it back inside as a friendly observer develops a new *conscious center* around which remaining parts of the self eventually become integrated. Whenever Alex was able to accomplish this task, his doubts continued to pass through awareness. Alex no longer identified with them, but simply observed them consciously and impartially. This process of *self-observation* is a vital tool for remaining detached within from events which otherwise would disquiet or disrupt the self. It is likewise a tool for actively promoting conscious living and inner security.

Conscious observation of the self, or self-observation, is the path toward developing a conscious, integrated self, one able to directly experience and have accurate knowledge of the many facets of the inner life. It allows us to integrate the self around a conscious center, and so to live consciously, fully conscious, fully observing, in the moment. Directing the focus of attention involves three interrelated aspects: focusing attention inwards, refocusing attention outwards, and, finally, dividing attention back upon itself through experiencing while simultaneously observing one's experience. Learning how to consciously direct the focus of attention is one of the principal tools for creating a conscious self, a self able to consciously *experience* inner events, *name* those events accurately, *own* them, *observe* them, and finally *detach* from them. These are the five key steps toward living consciously.

Imagery

Our final consideration in developing a conscious self is the process of visual *imagery*. We have all had waking daydreams in our lives comprising streams of visual images. Imagery is an internal process we can actively engage in. We simply close our eyes and wait for a visual image to spontaneously appear. We can watch this stream of visual imagery as a series of scenes flashing by.

Another thing we can do with imagery is *enter* it. One of us remembers vividly how as a boy he would walk home after a Saturday movie and replay it all. He would not only see it once again as he walked home but he would enter its world. It was all around him, happening.

Visual imagery can be a profound experience when we visualize events in fantasy and thereby experience them as real, as though in fact they had actually just occurred. The imagery process is an inherent function of the self though some individuals have easier access to it than others.

We can use imagery to *differentiate* feelings, needs, drives, or purposes; that is, experience, name, and own them. For example, we can run through in fantasy what it is we might be needing emotionally at a particular moment in time. By allowing ourselves to actively imagine, for example, "If I could have anything I needed right now, what would it be?" we can begin to put words together with our own inner experience. In this way we learn to distinguish among our interpersonal needs, our drives, and our feelings. Imagery is a way of recontacting these inner states, experiencing them more fully and, ultimately, making them conscious. The very same thing is true regarding our purposes. We can use imagery to aid us in discovering our guiding dreams, what truly matters most to us in living. By knowing our dreams, those essential goals we are living for, we discover renewed purpose and meaning to our lives.

Another way imagery can be utilized is through discharging intense feelings such as anger. It is vital to allow ourselves the full expression of feelings and impulses internally while placing the necessary control at the *boundary* between ourselves and the world. It is even psychologically healthy to allow ourselves destructive or hurtful fantasies with the full knowledge that they *are*, and must remain, fantasies. Imagining oneself actually doing hurt, violence, or damage is healthy because the fantasy engages our imagination, makes the experience real, and thereby safely discharges the affect.

The impulse to destroy, hurt, or kill is as human as the impulse to protect, create, or care. What allows us to make the choice is our ability to consciously know about, effectively channel, and ultimately control our violent urges. We are more likely to know about them at their earliest beginnings if we allow them into conscious fantasy. We are then less impelled to carry them further into action. In this way imagery can mediate, discharge, and help manage natural destructive urges.

One of the tools is looking to the source of those impulses to hurt someone back. Our human impulses to do violence are apt to be triggered either by intense shame-humiliation or else by a condition of powerlessness. These are the principal sources of violence.

Individuals who do not allow themselves to know about their potentially destructive impulses are the ones most likely to act them out. Only when such impulses are registered consciously do we have an opportunity to harmlessly discharge them while consciously controlling their behavioral expression and looking for the source of our impulse to hurt or destroy.

The point of control ought not to reside within the self, as when we forbid or silence some feeling, need, or impulse. Rather, we ought to exercise control at the boundary between the self and the outer world. Some years ago the son of one of us told his father that he had just had a bad thought about him. His father replied, "Oh, okay, but I don't happen to think there are any bad thoughts." The boy answered, " I just thought of the house falling down on you." Since he looked angry, father and son sat down and talked. Father explained to the boy that all feelings inside of us, all the thoughts, fantasies, or impulses, were natural and good. They are all a valid part of us. It is fine to *feel like* hurting someone, but he just can not *do* it. That is where we exercise control. Then his father told him about his own occasional fantasies of roasting certain individuals in the fireplace. That allowed the boy freedom to experience his own impulses while learning both how to discharge them safely and, equally importantly, *where* to exercise conscious control. Such a view runs counter to certain value systems or religious teachings, but denying our nature can never lead to psychological health or self-esteem.

Imagery has also been widely employed as a means of discharging the sexual drive. Sexual fantasy, whether alone or in conjunction with masturbation or intercourse, provides one outlet for discharging sexual impulses or tension. This is especially useful when one has consciously decided, as a result of other commitments, not to express those sexual impulses directly. We know one woman who was deeply ashamed of using fantasy when she and her husband made love. She felt it was wrong to imagine someone else touching her, and believed no one else had such fantasies. She was relieved to find out she was not alone. In fact, because fantasy directly recruits excitement affect, fantasy is both useful and necessary to sexual pleasure in any relationship over time.

Any time we are faced with a new situation that is sufficiently uncertain or threatening, we can run it through our fantasy life to become more familiar with it. By actively imagining ourselves through the ordeal we become *prepared* for it. When we enter into the imagery, it is as though we have experienced the situation in actuality.

Whenever a situation frightens us, we need to ask: "What's the very *worst* thing that could happen?" As soon as we can *name* our dread, our anxiety lessens. Naming confers power over our fear. Then we can figure out ways of coping with it should our worst fear actually occur. We can even play out the situation in fantasy and see ourselves cope with it by various means. Imagery is preparation for action, for life.

We can use imagery to try out an unfamiliar situation or a new behavior. We can also use it to assist us in deciding about a major life choice, such as career, job, life-style, or marriage. By actively imagining ourselves in the situation as vividly as possible, we can discover how well it suits us. This cannot ever provide certainty about our choices but it can meaningfully inform us about them. We never have all the information needed or available to guide us at those inevitable turning points of life and there is no substitute for trying new things to know if they are right for us. That test can only be made directly through our own experience over time. Nevertheless, imagery can inform our choices and teach us about ourselves.

Imagery can also heal or restore the self. In the previous chapter we explored how recontacting our inner child through imagery actively promoted eventual integration. This was a vital way of utilizing imagery to restore the self. We can go further and actually replay previously traumatic events in active imagery and then reparent ourselves through them, enabling inner wounds to heal. We can give ourselves more positive and freeing messages which are likely to become internalized as new attitudes about self. While we can never erase our personal history, imagery is a profound tool for transcending it.

And finally, imagery is another tool for detachment or letting go. One woman described a place on the northern shores of Lake Michigan where all cares leave her. By vividly imagining herself there—feeling the warmth of the sun, smelling the fresh breeze off the lake, listening to the waves wash the shore, seeing the birds and clouds sailing by, listening to the distant laughter of children down the endless beach—the experience becomes as real as if she were actually there. After five or ten minutes on this fantasy vacation, she has been able to let go of whatever tensions or concerns have preoccupied her, emerging renewed and refreshed. This is a tool we can use anywhere, anytime we need to detach or let go.

As we have seen, imagery is a vital process of the self which has many uses, all of which aim at increasing conscious living within the self.

Translating Theory Into Action:
Creating Tools

The following tools are translations of the foregoing principles into action. In order to master them, consistent practice over time will be necessary. Experiment to see which ones are right for you.

Tool #1: Consultation With Self[11]

Set aside ten minutes once a day to consult self. Focus attention inwards to experience inner events consciously: How am I *feeling* now? What am I *needing* emotionally? How is my *body* reacting? What are my dreams, my *purposes?* Experience, name, and then own each of these distinct parts of the self as natural and valid.

Tool #2: Meditation

This is a one-point focusing of attention. Set aside fifteen minutes, relax your body, quiet yourself, close your eyes and focus your attention on one point: a sound, your breathing, or counting from one to four on exhaling. Then allow all feelings, thoughts, memories, or fantasies simply to come into awareness and then to pass through awareness. The purpose is to learn to let go of, or detach from, the contents of consciousness by focusing all attention on one point. Meditation is a way of quieting the self that teaches us how to develop inner detachment.

Tool #3: Bubble Meditation[12]

Close your eyes and imagine yourself sitting quietly at the bottom of a clear lake. Much as large bubbles slowly rise through water, picture each thought or feeling as a bubble rising into the space you can observe, passing through and then out of this space. Allow seven or eight seconds for each bubble to pass into and out of visual awareness. When you have a thought or feeling, simply observe it for this time period, encased in its "bubble," until it passes out of your visual space. Then calmly wait for the next one and observe it similarly. Do not explore, follow up or think about a bubble, just observe it. Allow fifteen minutes for this meditation. With practice this will teach us one way of detaching from or letting go of unsettling, anxious, or stressful events.

Tool #4: Letting Go Through Imagery

Select a comfortable sitting or reclining position. Close your eyes, and think about a place that you have been before that allows you to fully detach or let go. (It should be a quiet environment, perhaps the seashore or the mountains. If you can not think of a real place, then create one in your mind.) Now imagine that you are actually in this place. Imagine that you are seeing all the colors, hearing the sounds, smelling the aromas. Just lie back, and enjoy your soothing, rejuvenating environment. Feel the peacefulness, the calmness and imagine your whole body and mind being renewed and refreshed. After five to ten minutes, slowly open your eyes and stretch. Remember, you can instantly return to your place whenever you desire, and experience a peacefulness and calmness in body and mind.

Tool #5: Refocusing Attention

Practice letting go of, or detaching from negative feelings, mistakes, or failings by consciously refocusing attention outwards. It is fine to take something useful from our mistakes, but then we must find a way to let go of them. Attention can be refocused into external sensory experience such as listening to music, going for a walk, or even reading murder mysteries. Attention can also be refocused onto a physical task such as jogging, swimming, bicycling, or even cleaning closets. It is the conscious refocusing of attention by a sheer effort of will which accomplishes the much-needed letting go inside.

TOOL #6: SELF-OBSERVATION

The task here is learning how to divide attention by holding a part of the self back inside as a friendly *observer*. The observing part of the self develops a new *conscious center* which then can integrate all of the remaining parts of the self around it. It is perhaps the most difficult task of all to remember to observe the self consciously in the moment of our experience. Simply attempting to *observe* our own feelings of discomfort or pain enables us to detach from them by stepping out of the experience even while we are in it. The key here is remembering, when caught in the net of our reactions, to step back from or outside of them, to simply observe them consciously with a detached and friendly eye. Twice a day, remember to keep a part of the self back inside as a friendly observer, or simply observe yourself while engaged in a repetitive task such as washing dishes. And whenever you feel taken over by a particular emotion or reaction, step outside of it and attempt to observe it impartially, as though from a distance.

TOOL #7: FUTURE SCENES OF PURPOSE

We need to know our guiding dreams, and also what we are expecting or looking for from each and every sphere of life we are *invested* in, that matters to us. This is a way of consciously identifying the central guiding dreams connected to our life's varied pursuits. We must also know how realistic our dreams and expectations are, how well they match reality. Questions to ask ourselves are: Why did I choose this particular kind of work? What motivates me to do it? What am I looking for from marriage or family? Which is more important, career or family, or are both important? Do I like and respect my work? Do I enjoy my work, is it fun?

Begin by observing consciously the recurring dramas you imagine yourself enacting in the future. What are the parts you see yourself playing over and over? What are your favorite dreams and daydreams? What are your principal, guiding scenes? By observing your recurring dreams, you make conscious the scenes in the future in which you cast yourself as hero.

Next, identify three or four key things you are looking for or expecting from each guiding dream in various areas of living: *Work/ Career, Relationships, Marriage/Partnerships, Parenting, Other Interests.* Be as specific and concrete as possible when identifying the expectations connected to each of your dreams. It will require much soul-searching and consultation with self to make these dreams and accompanying expectations conscious.

After you have identified your scenes and expectations, ask yourself which ones are actually *in your control* to attain and which ones are out of your control. Then look at which scenes and expectations are *realistic* given the particular situation concerned. Finally, with regard to each of your identified scenes and expectations, ask yourself *how much is enough* in order to feel a basic satisfaction with self.

The Tools in Action:
Experiences From the Course

Learning to live consciously requires work: effortful practice over time. This has been borne out repeatedly in the course as partipants are challenged to use particular tools in their own lives. Tina kicked off the discussion of *consultation with self:* "I do a periodic check at least twice a day for five minutes. Because of this I am becoming much more aware of my feelings and feel more alive and excited about living. A lot of these feelings haven't always been pleasant lately but they are real and are a very important part of me and my life right now. I do believe things are getting better." Diane continued the discussion, adding a variation to the tool which suited her better: "What I've begun doing is writing in a journal how I feel throughout the day about encounters I run across each day. I'm doing this because I have a difficult time just sitting down and asking myself how I feel. This way I can see all the mixtures of feelings I have inside me." Howard described a different variation: "I combine this consulting self tool with meditation. Concentration or meditation has allowed me to more closely monitor my feelings at any particular moment and I seem to be able to more spontaneously feel and label the emotions I feel as I feel them, rather than having to wait for a period of time before becoming conscious of how I might have felt two-to-three days ago. I find myself living more in the present, and less in the past or future. In meditation I practice labeling and naming thoughts I have. This not only helps me own them, but it allows me to detach myself somewhat from them, and then I have the option to experience these feelings or not experience them." Awareness of self has been enlarged for these individuals through use of the tool, consulting self.

Practice over time results not only in mastery of this tool but in self-discovery as well. Rudy reported the following reactions over a three week period: "I do this most days. It is moderately to very helpful. I don't always feel I have access to my feelings. Sometimes it's depressing because it seems like many needs aren't being filled. Perhaps I should try to plan positive action on the basis of the insights I get through the self consultations." A week later: "I find it helpful but I'm having lots of trouble establishing a habit of doing it regularly. Feelings and future purposes are the easiest to formulate." Again, a week later: "I do this regularly. The feeling and purpose parts are the most useful. The feeling part helps me pin down anxieties that I'm not conscious of but have been chasing me all day. The purpose part helps me to remember to prioritize activities and do things I'm satisfied with myself for." Randy reported the following reactions over a four-week period: "I try to write these down each day but don't regularly. I do often consult myself during the day and it helps me realize 'where I'm coming from. . . .' Feel this one is important though I still often have a hard time pinpointing the feelings. Distress seems to be where my negative feelings usually go. I have a hard time with anger, even identifying it, as I don't think I've allowed myself this one. . . . Can identify feelings better. Anger is still the hard one for me. My greatest need now is for relationships. I am cultivating the old and working on new ones and I'm 'sharing' this class with them. . . . I identified *anger* today! I realized I had retreated from it as I often do." Through use of the tool, Randy consciously recontacted his own anger which, for him, was a significant step.

Through practice, Rudy and Randy overcame initial difficulties using the tool and reached a deeper level of self-understanding. Others experienced varying degrees of difficulty with the tool as well as varying insights about themselves. Rita observed: "Although I've been practicing this one I seem to sometimes have problems with accurate naming of specific feelings and future purposes. I am, however, getting real good at detecting my body messages." A week later, Rita said: "I'm still warring inside over which set of purposes to adhere to, the old one or a newer one. Still doing well with bodily states and needs." The next week: "I initially had more problems with this one. Now it seems to come a bit easier, especially the body area."

While listening to her body came readily for Rita, Sarah had a different experience in this area as well as generally greater difficulty with the tool itself: "I suppose I *should* do this but never have on a systematic basis. I think I am especially confused about 'needs.' I'm afraid I haven't figured out what my personal needs are but I think a lot about the needs of other people, or at least what I perceive as their needs." A few weeks later, Sarah's experience with the tool shifted somewhat: "I've been trying to do lots (for me) of swimming lately and have begun to try to be aware of my *body* as I swim. I think I, as many other people, have been brainwashed to think my body is something 'bad' to which I should pay little attention (except to adorn it with clothes, make-up, etc., as dictated by the media). Becoming truly aware of my body and how it feels, what it needs, is a new experience." Carol's experience paralleled Sarah's: "I am having a slightly difficult time with this tool because when I really need to listen to my body is when my defenses are the strongest against my doing this. But the battle has just begun." Two weeks later, Carol reported: "I've placed all or most of my energy into using the tool this week. I'm still unclear about my body's language but I've become more conscious that these needs are there and they are always presenting themselves. Since I haven't been conscious before, they've been ignored and I'm sure I've been feeling the effects in other areas of my life."

In using the tool consistently over a one-to-three week period, two course participants contacted unexplored realms of feeling. Susan reported: "Found some real loneliness inside me. I thought long and hard about why I'm so sad, and have been for a long time. . . . Spent time evaluating my needs and feelings and my expectations concerning my relationship with my boyfriend. . . . Went further with last night's consultation. . . . I found this to be painful today. I didn't want to pursue or dwell on my feelings because they were painful. . . . Really got into this. Cried because I felt like I have needs which aren't going to be met for a long time. . . . Felt better about it today. Strategized ways to get my needs met and to live with those that won't be met for awhile." Margo described: "I know my needs but don't have words to describe my feelings. . . . I've discerned that one of my feelings is frustration, because I'm still adapting to a new environment. . . . Frustration continues. However, I'm beginning to see possible outcomes of this sequence—there's hope! . . . I'm really focusing in on what feelings I have and what needs must be met. . . . There seems to be an area of myself which I don't want to face, perhaps my reason for not adapting here yet—still looking for some feelings. . . . Today I talked about some of my feelings with a friend. This was a big stride for me since I usually don't disclose for a long time after I meet people. . . . Some of the feelings I've found are loneliness, confusion, and stress. I also know I'm feeling this way—which is good. . . . I've decided that I need more from my classes than I'm getting. . . . Still feeling a little lonely but I'm beginning to adjust and move on. . . . I want to see into the future—where will I be? . . . I need to see my boyfriend more. . . . I'm finding myself in a larger perspective and seeking options. . . . I wondered if my boyfriend is really at the core of my happiness."

Susan and Margo each practiced using the tool on a regular, almost daily basis. Through this process, more of their inner experience became known to them. They became conscious of particular feelings or needs which previously had remained obscure and further learned to fit inner events to words through accurate naming.

Consultation with self—encompassing the three steps of experiencing, naming, and owning—promotes conscious living but requires the capacity for detachment to complete it. The ability to detach from and, hence, let go of particular feelings is vital to psychological health. Rita reported the following reactions to the *refocusing attention* tool: "I've done this one a number of times over the past seven days. I've refocused attention onto tasks that are physical, like housekeeping chores, walking, dancing, cooking, etc." A week later, Rita added the following: "I'm starting to develop a longer refocus span of attention but at times it takes a lot of effort." Again, a week later: "I'm still doing fine. I found it helped to have a list of let-go activities already prepared to choose from." Randy described the following experiences: "I walk or ride my bike to and from work. I feel much better when I get to work or get home. I also have time to talk with myself." Two weeks later, he reported: "I had a 'run-in' with an employee this week. I faced it and then let it go. It would come back but I would let it go again." Tina's experience paralleled that of Rita and Randy: "I have consciously refocused my attention by doing yard work and then going for a two-mile walk. I did this twice last week and it helped."

Stuart reported increased difficulty with learning to let go: "Not too good here. I swim and distract myself and tell myself to let go, but there's something in me that's equally insistent on making me hold on to and be aware of the feelings (fear and inadequacy) I would like to let go of." Yet Rudy felt otherwise: "I've consciously refocused my attention onto a task when I've been upset several times. It's very helpful when I do it."

Refocusing attention is one tool for accomplishing detachment and *meditation* is another. Ruth spoke about her reactions over the course of several weeks: "I feel that the meditation and imagery tools were most helpful and beneficial to me. They provided me with the means to let go of stress and irritating thoughts at least until I could ponder them more rationally. With these tools, I could relax, something I hadn't been able to do in a long time. The happiness lists also helped to ease depression within me. It really works!" Tina joined in: "I've been combining the meditation and imagery tools. I do this at least two times a day and usually three times for fifteen minutes. These have helped me gain a great deal of inner peace."

Discussion shifted to *letting go through imagery.* Carmen led off: "This tool was very helpful to me when I was overwhelmed with guilt and hurt from a relationship that was falling apart. It helped me cope until I could get more control of my emotions." Rita joined in: "I've used this one quite a bit lately and found it to be useful as a tension reliever. I've also found particular stimuli lately evoking the image, smells especially. Because of my recent pleasant experience in a lakeside setting, I've substituted this image setting for an old one I was using." Cathy responded with her variation: "Rather than imagine an environment with sounds and colors, I imagine a certain person I know and have a conversation or a fight. This helps me the most with letting go of being afraid. I find it harder to picture myself in a relaxed environment and let go that way."

The foregoing examples illustrate how different individuals in the course actually utilized the various tools in their on-going, every-day lives. Certain tools come easier than others for particular individuals.

And initial difficulties often give way, with consistent practice, to increasing ability. Individuals also discovered which of the various tools for accomplishing detachment worked best for them. Self-discovery flowed from mastery of the tools. Rudy gained access to his feelings while Randy discovered his anger and Sarah became aware of her body. Each learned to live more consciously.

Developing a Conscious Self

The challenge we have been considering is creating a truly *conscious self.* To accomplish this rather momentous developmental task, we must learn to live consciously, moment-by-moment, through all of life's endeavors. Living consciously means being fully present, fully aware, in the moment. Living consciously means being able to *experience* inner events, *name* them accurately, *own* them, *observe* them, and finally, *detach* from them. It is no simple task. Considerable practice over time will be required of us if we are to attain it. And never do we become perfect at it either. We are always in process.

CHAPTER 4

Power and Shame in Interpersonal Relations

If developing a conscious competent self challenges our confidence, skill, and determination, establishing satisfying human relationships presents no less a challenge. We are not born knowing how to be a competent self; neither are we born knowing how to navigate the human world. Our ability to make meaningful, if not lasting, connection with other people requires a set of skills which must be learned through practice. Having relationships is indeed a craft which must be worked at actively if it is to be learned at all.

One dimension of the craft encompasses all of the work we have been considering: conscious knowledge of self. We must have free access to our affects (feelings), needs, drives, and purposes. We must be able to experience, name, and own all of the different parts of the self within us as distinguishable parts of an integrated self. We must live consciously within ourselves as well as in that outer world of people and things, seeing the reality of people and situations confronting us as objectively and honestly as possible. Matching our expectations with reality, as we have considered this skill earlier, lies at the heart of the craft of interpersonal relating.

Another important dimension of the craft involves a sharpening of awareness concerning just what this business of relationships precisely is all about. Why do we have relationships at all? What motivates us to make connection with others or bond together?

A Developmental Perspective

Let us enlarge our focus and consider the developmental life context of the individual as an important shaper of our relationships.

First of all, we move through a series of five primary interpersonal settings, beginning with the *family* into which we are born. That is our first experience with the human world, including parents, siblings, grandparents as well as others who become significant throughout our early years. At this early phase certain developmental tasks condition the nature of our interpersonal relating. These tasks include separation from mother, acquisition of language, developing autonomy and competence, and establishing separate relationships with each parent.

The developmental tasks in which we are engaged continue to shape the kind of relationships we seek to form as well as our changing needs from those relationships. As middle and later childhood unfold, we move into two new primary interpersonal settings, *school* and the *peer group*. Our interpersonal realm has enlarged itself; peers become signficant to us as well as teachers. Relating effectively with peers takes on vital importance, culminating in finding a same-sex chum, as Harry Stack Sullivan has observed. Play evolves into companionship and, later, into the pursuit of intimacy.

With the dawn of adolescence, the peer group's role becomes especially heightened. Attachment to the family is shaken loose and eventually redirected to the peer group itself. The storm of adolescence disrupts the previous equilibrium attained in our relationships. In part this is due to the extreme self-consciousness and exposure suddenly unleashed by the profound bodily changes now besetting us. Adolescence is a developmental epoch during which the affect of shame becomes universally heightened.[1] The storm involves something else as well: separation from the family. It is precisely through that growing loyalty, even allegiance, to peers that we are at all able to separate. Developing intimacy and integrating sexuality share the focus along with separation from the family as the central developmental tasks of adolescence.

There is a frequently observed transitional phase between adolescence and early adulthood which involves a quest for freedom and independence. Just as adolescents become legally adult and move out of the only home they have known, many often experience an intense yearning to be free of obligations. This striving can involve a refusal to commit to anything, whether relationships or even a career path. Or it may become expressed in a need to experiment widely, to travel on one's own, or otherwise break away from previously accepted values and traditions. Whether all individuals experience this freedom phase or only particular ones is by no means certain. And whether this striving for freedom is partially a function of the extended adolescence and apprenticeship required by a highly specialized, technological society must also remain an open question. What is important to remember is openly acknowledging its presence, for this quest for freedom will profoundly affect the kind of relationships we seek with other individuals. It is foolish, for example, to attempt a commitment to another person while one is still yearning to be utterly free and independent, not responsible to anyone. Many young people need to go through this freedom phase, literally need to *have* their freedom, before they are ready to make essential choices about career, lifestyle, or marriage. It is equally true that many individuals either prolong this phase or else remain stuck there. On the other hand, individuals who happen to bypass this phase frequently will experience the yearning for freedom surfacing later in life, often after they have made essential choices concerning career, marriage, and family. Though many attempt it, there is no good way at that point to go back and experience one's freedom in entirety without simultaneously missing the current round of developmental tasks one ought now to be engaging. One would be forever chasing after past needs and attempting to catch up.

If development proceeds on course, separation culminates in attaining or establishing one's own *separate identity*. That is the hallmark of early adulthood, becoming a self in one's own right. The developmental tasks of this stage involve making a series of essential choices regarding such matters as career, relationships, lifestyle, including marriage or other forms of partnership, parenting, and discovering guiding purposes in living. We now move into two additional primary interpersonal settings, the *work setting* and possibly our own *marriage and/or family*. Through these essential choices we define the self we are and eventually attain a separate identity. We discover our own unique way of going about the task which life hands us all.

Mid-life presents us with a unique crisis of purpose. Spiritual concerns and renewing purpose re-emerge as we move toward completion of our life-work. Even later, we begin to review our major life choices along the way to see whether we have lived well. Facing old age and acceptance of death round out the series of developmental tasks which stretch throughout the life cycle.

The foregoing discussion of developmental tasks is not intended to be comprehensive, but rather to provide a meaningful context for viewing the evolving nature of interpersonal relationships as life itself unfolds. The varying developmental tasks we are actively engaged in will continue to affect in important ways the kind of relationships we seek.

Dimensions of a Relationship

There are several key dimensions which distinguish relationships. The first of these reflects that set of primary interpersonal needs comprising the *need system* discussed in Chapter Three. Our need for relationship itself is among these, our need to feel special and wanted, our need for human understanding. We also have needs for belonging, to identify with someone or with a group. We have other needs for touching and holding. We have different needs to nurture others, to give to or care about another person. And we have needs for affirmation, embracing valuing, respect, admiration, and recognition. These needs are the heart of vulnerability. When we *need* in this fashion, we open ourselves to another. Through our primary needs, the quality of caring unfolds.

These needs are *security needs,* for they are directly linked to our sense of inner security. Insofar as our primary needs are responded to appropriately and sufficiently, we feel secure. This is as true for children as it is for adults. Relationships in which we look for security needs are *security relationships.*

Companionship constitutes a second order of relationships which reflects a different quality of relating. Security needs are not necessarily at the forefront here; the level of relating is one of *sharing* as opposed to *needing.* For example, people form attachments around either work or play activities. The purpose largely is the sharing of interests held in common.

The third level of relationships involves all those which are *obligatory,* ones we have not chosen to be in. We find these in school among classmates and teachers. We find them at work among colleagues, co-workers, and supervisors. And we find them among parents, siblings, and relatives. Certainly many of these may indeed be warm, loving, or supportive relationships. Yet the nature of these relationships inevitably involves elements of obligation.

The final level of relationships involves *sexuality,* a unique dimension of relating which can enter into any of the other types of relationships. Sexual relationships engage an added dimension to our interpersonal relating which is usefully distinguished from security, companionship, or obligatory relationships.

These four dimensions reflect differences with regard to the quality of relating, level of intensity, and degree of emotional investment. They also reflect differences regarding our basic expectations from the particular relationship concerned. We look for different things in a companionship relationship than we do from a security relationship. Hence, it is useful to distinguish our relationships according to the set of expectations we have of them.

Relationship Guidelines:
Learning to be Self-Preservative

Relationships involve the mutual expression of *affect* and *need.* The blend of enjoyment affect with such needs as identification and touching/holding creates the experience of love or caring. When such needs go unmet or fail to be understood, or when barriers arise to the continued mutual expression of positive affect, then relationships become impaired. The single greatest impediment to the pursuit of intimacy is shame. This chapter is about some of the choices we have for coping more effectively with our relationships. It is difficult to write about such matters and simultaneously preserve some of the flow, some of the natural ease and comfort which indeed can be experienced between many individuals. Relationships are by no means always difficult nor even necessarily fraught with danger. Occasionally a relationship blossoms quite naturally with seemingly little effort on our part. Keeping passion alive, bringing caring into our work and into our relationships challenge us all.

The ideas we will be considering are not intended to be used in some calculating manner but, instead, to eventually blend and flow throughout our relating. Power must be warmed by caring and released through our vulnerability. Remembering to be vulnerable wisely is the goal we are after.

Relationships are also living things to be nurtured. Sometimes they do become impaired though many can be eventually restored. There are times when we continue to blunder or repeat patterns which undo us. When we have become vulnerable unwisely, remember that we also have the ability to restore ourselves from our hurts. If faced honestly, we grow through pain.

This chapter is not about the joys of bonding and its cherished successes, but about its pitfalls and possible ways to avoid them. As you read, remember to provide for yourself the context of warmth, of caring, and of compassion. Remember as you read to consider each thought or idea as something to be filtered through our humanity.

It is difficult to teach these ideas without making them sound calculating, but interpersonal relating needs to be *conscious.* In order to learn a new set of skills, we must first break them into specific steps which can be identified, accurately named, practiced, and eventually integrated. Our goal is learning to relate more consciously. Caring is one dimension of that craft and power is another.

THE GUIDELINES

Remembering that each person is a package of " + 's" and " − 's," a combination of vital strengths along with some weaknesses, is one of the most important considerations to bear in mind when undertaking the craft of relationships. Each of us is a package of unique qualities, with a preferred mode of relating. We may even experience quite different sets of needs in relation to other humans; we bring to our relationships varying sets of expectations.

It is essential to learn how to *consciously observe* people in order to see the unique reality of that particular individual. For example, if we look for emotional closeness in our relationships, then we must be able to objectively observe others to see if they also desire and are capable of closeness. Otherwise we may end up in the rather awkward position of expecting a cat to sing *Faust.* We must consciously observe each person in order to know just what kind of people we are dealing with.

Capacity for closeness or intimacy is certainly one key dimension to assess. There are others equally vital to forming a satisfying relationship. Some individuals relate in a fairly genuine and honest fashion while others do not. Some relate emotionally while others prefer to relate intellectually or cognitively. Some are capable of genuine warmth; others are only superficially friendly while actually hostile underneath. Some are dependable because their behavior matches their words while others behave in just the opposite fashion. Some are capable of sharing the power in a relationship while others seek to hoard the power. Some are capable of commitment in a relationship and others avoid it. Some are capable of vulnerability and others refuse ever to become vulnerable; doing so is too dangerous for them.

Through the process of conscious objective observation, which we will translate into action later, we gradually discover other people's preferred style of relating, unique qualities as a person, basic values in living, and other vital capacities. It is certainly no easy task to accomplish. Involved here is learning a set of skills, a way of approaching relationships very consciously, so that our own needs and expectations of a relationship can be matched with the reality of that particular individual.

Above all else, we must remember to be *self-preservative* in our relationships. Otherwise it is too easy to end up feeling powerless or resentful. We must work consciously with ourselves in order to identify what we want and do not want in each and every relationship we undertake. We can also care about another's feelings, needs, and happiness without necessarily feeling responsible for them. We must also know our natural *limits* in our relationships and forthrightly exercise our inalienable right to say "No" to others. Just because someone wishes us to engage in a particular activity does not mean we ought to unless we have first *consulted ourselves* to see if we truly want to and are comfortable so doing. This is as true for going out somewhere as it is for engaging in sex. One young woman was called by an old friend newly returned to town who wanted to spend an evening together. Being in the midst of exams, she did not have the time to go out with him but could spare time to visit over a cup of coffee. In saying this, she was being honest about her own limits and, hence, self-preservative.

Being self-preservative is certainly only the half of it. Relationships require a capacity to care about the other person's needs and feelings as well. Each must be willing to give a little, to compromise some, so that each person's needs are taken willingly into consideration by the other. The point, however, is that we also remember to consider our own feelings and needs so that we do not sacrifice ourselves. Through caring about ourselves as well as the other person, a mutually satisfying relationship evolves.

We do have a right and duty to ourselves to preserve our comfort and must, at certain times, be prepared to gently or firmly educate others about how to have a relationship with us. We do this by saying openly and honestly what our wants and needs are as well as sticking firm to our own limits. Not wanting to do something with another can be a sufficient reason not to, requiring no further explanation. Consider how many times your not wanting to do something has been met with, "Well, *why* not?" We are taught that not wanting to is insufficient; we must have valid reasons for justifying our reluctance. However, wanting to or not wanting to is precisely the reason and we need never feel obligated to explain further. To choose is to say "yes" or "no," to want or not want. These are translations of the concept of choice into action.

Of course, there is another equally vital side to this question. There are inevitable circumstances which occur within caring relationships when we are called upon to do things which we do not really want to do. Such is the case when, for example, we are called upon to help out a friend who needs us. These are times when we may actually choose to set aside our own wants.

Through stating our limits in a relationship we also discover whether the other is capable of respecting our rights and, hence, is both willing and able to share the power. Alternatively, we may find the other resentful about not getting his or her own way, or else manipulative. Manipulativeness is an emotionally dishonest attempt to get what one wants or to control others. One of the prevalent means for manipulating others is through inducing guilt. This is done by behaving in a disappointed or hurt fashion when the other does not behave as one wishes. Hence, as discussed earlier, it is crucial to distinguish between guilt as a disappointment in self and guilt as a disappointment in someone else. That is the only way to know whether we have, in fact, done some regrettable deed in our own eyes or, instead, we are simply not behaving as others might wish us to. Whenever we are faced with the choice of disappointing ourselves or disappointing another, it is preferable to disappoint that other person in any matter of importance. We can listen to the other's feelings of hurt, anger, and disappointment and also understand their feelings without having to do anything about them.

We must remember that each one of us will at times actually be a disappointment to others. This will be true in all of our human relationships, even our best or most important ones. It is a reality to be expected, not something to be avoided or dreaded. Just as we need to feel we can *fail at something* without being a *failure,* we need to give ourselves permission to *disappoint others* without labeling ourselves a *disappointment.*

Much of what has been said here might raise the charge of selfishness. Being selfish is not necessarily abhorrent but, rather, quite natural and even positive. We must know our own needs in whatever pursuits we undertake. And we ought to get something out of it, a return for our labors, or why bother. Even our most altruistic of endeavors are motivated by selfishness of a sort, by our deepest needs to give, to nurture, and to care. Selfishness that is in one's own behalf, truly in care of self, must be distinguished from selfishness that is at the expense of others.

The more self-preservative we are, the more we actually will, in truth, have to give to others. The freer we are to give or not give, the more we will want to.

As hard as it may be to believe, some people will not like us. That is a reality of life. When we feel that people do not like us, we often experience shame, wondering "What's wrong with me?" Because of shame, we sometimes persist in trying to make that person like us, even when we do not like the individual. We will *not* like every person we encounter. To expect that we will like everyone or that everyone will like us are unrealistic expectations which inevitably lead to shame and disappointment. Instead of worrying about the ones we do not like, we ought to look instead to where we are indeed liked. We ought to ask ourselves how we feel about the other before worrying, in the first place, about how the other feels towards us. Often, though not always, the people who do not like us are the same people that we do not especially like. We have to remember to take a hard conscious look at the other person in order to decide how we, in truth, feel about him or her. We cannot ever *make* another like us; that is not in our power.

Another factor we must be cognizant of is the impact we have on others. Each one of us creates particular feelings in others by virtue of our behavior and it is useful to know what they are. We must be willing to understand and honestly own our impact on others, whether intended or not. For example, introverts, who tend to be quiet and hard to know, have a clear impact on others: they generally leave people anxious precisely because they do not talk as openly about what is going on inside of them. Hence, others are left more in the dark.

In any relationship, however significant or satisfying, there will be many times when we have understanding, caring, and emotional support to give to the other person. There are also times when we do *not* have it to give emotionally speaking because our own barrel is empty. We ourselves are feeling "needy." A basic rule is never to give out of *deprivation* or else we will end up resentful or angry about it. It is better for all concerned to give only out of *abundance*. The way to monitor our own inner supply of emotional stores is, again, through regular *consultation with self*. If we ignore our own inner state and attempt to give out of deprivation, not only will we reap a harvest of resentment but what we are giving is, in truth, not worth having. It is more like poison or sour milk because our resentment is also transmitted, and will spoil whatever we are attempting to give the other.

As a final consideration, it is useful to be extremely wary of "instant intimacy" or attempts at rushing a relationship. Good relationships take slow and careful building over many months. It is necessary to observe the other person consciously in a variety of situations over time in order to know just what kind of individual he or she is. It also takes time and repeated contact to develop ease and comfort with one another. And it takes time to build the day-by-day supports which make any relationship work. Six months to a year is a more realistic expectation regarding the length of time needed to feel a sense of certainty about a new relationship. Intimacy or caring are not instant, but grow naturally in their own time. It is wiser not to attempt to rush them because relationships which become too close too quickly often blow apart. Sound relationships evolve gradually and require conscious attention. Living consciously in the world is the best safeguard.

When the foregoing guidelines become second-nature to us, they will surface as gentle signals in the natural course of our relating to keep us in a position of equal power. These principles will echo softly within us, enabling us to navigate the world with greater competence. Then our ability to care will flourish more soundly. While it is important to care and often deeply so, we must always remember to be vulnerable wisely.

Becoming Self-Preservative:
A Case in Point

Let us take a closer look at the foregoing principles of relating in action. We will be focusing on how to become self-preservative with emphasis on such basic principles as choice, power, and living consciously.

Joan came to therapy with the first author immediately following a truly frightening incident in which she had felt so utterly depressed that she could not get out of bed the previous evening to prepare dinner for her daughter. Joan had always kept her own feelings inside and her pressing concerns to herself; there was no one in her present life to whom she turned for emotional support. She was also a single parent living with her two daughters to whom she was devoted. Her depression had been building for some time until the previous night's frightening incident had occurred, motivating Joan to finally seek assistance.

When her therapist first saw her, she was acutely depressed and on the verge of giving up hope. She felt there was nothing to live for. They worked to identify possible triggers for her depression and she related the following series of events. Eighteen months previously, she had divorced her husband and subsequently required major surgery. Then a sibling of hers was killed in a freak accident. Finally, her father suffered a heart attack. Joan began to wonder if she was just now beginning to experience consciously the emotional impact of that series of losses and disruptions in her life. This seemed quite likely to her therapist.

Apart from the very real absence of emotional support in her life, Joan's recent divorce seemed to be the principal continuing source of major difficulties. She still felt guilty and ashamed about divorcing her husband and depriving her children of a home with two parents. Hence, she had not as yet fully resolved this matter for herself. Furthermore, relatives on both sides of the family had continued to pressure her to become reconciled with her former husband, something he also had been pressuring her to agree to.

Joan's father was recovering well, and her own surgery was behind her. While the sudden death of her sibling was unfortunate, none of these events accounted for the continuation of Joan's feelings of depression, hopelessness, and deepening despair. Clearly, she had been feeling powerless and readily agreed that this was her underlying feeling state. Naming it accurately was a vital first step.

They then worked to make the roots of Joan's powerlessness conscious. Once they understood the sources of her feeling hopeless and helpless, they could figure out how to extricate her from this dangerous position.

One of the facts which surfaced early on was that Joan's mother had walked out on the family when Joan herself was a child. She had been raised by her father from that point on. Even before that event had occurred, Joan felt she could never please her mother, that no matter what she did or how she behaved, she was never good enough for mother. This was one source of her shame. And her mother's subsequent abandonment, for that was how it felt to Joan, only confirmed Joan's abiding sense of inner deficiency. This was proof there was something wrong with *her*.

Years later she married a man who behaved in ways that were irresponsible. He looked to Joan to make all the decisions, even to run interference for him at his job, to literally care for him the way a parent does for a child. He also engaged in a series of extramarital affairs, always promising to stop. Finally, Joan had had enough and, after considerable inner struggle, decided to opt for divorce, though she continued to feel there was something wrong with *her* for not being able to make their marriage work. The failures in her relationship with her mother left Joan susceptible to experiencing the breakup of her marriage as another personal failure, another confirmation of her shame. The recurring pressure from her ex-husband as well as many family members only confused her further and deepened her sense of shame about breaking up the family.

Her therapist helped Joan realize that she had indeed tried repeatedly to make her marriage work and, even further, that she herself truly felt she had *tried enough*. There was no sense in sacrificing her own well-being in the bargain. Besides, she knew she would never reconcile with her former husband. There was nothing left inside her that wanted to try again.

Realizing the impact of the failures in her relationship with her mother enabled Joan to see how susceptible she was, in one sense, to repeating a similar pattern in her marriage. She could not see the behavior of the other person objectively, but always experienced herself as the failure.

Once she came to realize the source of her longstanding sense of inner deficiency and the reality of the particular individual she had married, Joan was able to feel more at peace about the divorce. Gradually her depression began to lift, particularly after she started paying conscious attention to what triggered her recurring depressive bouts. Once her eyes were opened and she began to observe consciously the actual sequence of events which resulted in her becoming depressed once again, Joan was able to identify and report specific events in her present life which seemed to reactivate her depressive posture. Most notably, these seemed to follow current interactions either with her mother or else with her former husband, two of the individuals who had played so central a role in her life to date.

Joan continued to feel powerless, in the present, in relation to her mother and her ex-husband. After a long absence, her mother was pressuring Joan to have a relationship with her and to bring her granddaughters to visit more often. Yet the predominant message from her mother to Joan was really no different than it had been in childhood. If Joan called, her mother said she did not call enough or should visit more often. Basically, whatever Joan did was not enough or not good enough, reopening the old wound and stimulating her inner sense of deficiency.

What was to be done? Joan needed to consciously decide what she felt she owed her mother, considering what her mother gave her. After considerable soul searching, Joan realized that no matter what she gave, it was never enough. Therefore, she was going to give only what she truly wanted to, which was not very much. She had no real feeling at all for this person who was her biological mother. Joan decided she would simply behave towards her mother as though she were another adult. Her therapist offered Joan a *defense*. He suggested that whenever her mother gave the recurring message "You're not good enough," Joan could reply with "Apparently I'm a disappointment to you, but I do the best I can." It worked. Joan no longer felt helpless with her mother.

The situation with her former husband was much more complicated since interaction was indeed necessary to arrange or accommodate visitation with the children. Whenever she saw him, her ex-husband would again pressure her for a reconciliation, in response to which Joan again tried to explain herself. This only left her once more confused, guilty, and resentful. He would also intrude on her privacy with questions or accusations about her personal life. Joan had been feeling powerless to stop these intrusions, thinking that if she were pleasant and rational he would finally understand. All this accomplished was reinforcing the very pattern she abhorred.

When he came for the children, he would often come quite late at night and then claim it was too late to take them and couldn't he sleep there. If she said, "Get a motel room," he answered, "Well, I have no money." Then she would finally back down and allow him to sleep in the living room. In return for her kindness, he played the T.V. set all night, keeping her awake, and failed to leave in the morning with the children as planned. In fact, it was yet another day before he finally left, only after countless cross-examinations of Joan's comings and going, and pleas for reconciliation, all of course, for the good of the children. Needless to say, Joan was enraged by this time.

When he returned the children, often it was well past their bed-time; they were over-tired and crabby, which further enraged Joan. "Why couldn't he be more responsible?" she would rail. "Why should this time be any different from all the others?" her therapist would answer.

Other times he would ignore the children, fail to call them for long stretches of time, even fail to show up as expected. All of this was an apparent attempt to hurt Joan through the children because he knew he could get to her that way. Joan cared that her daughters had a father and a real relationship with him. Investing in that was pre-carious for Joan; it was not at all in her control. Since it mattered to her, he was able to abuse the power she inadvertently gave him. Whenever she resisted his pleas for reconciliation, he ignored the children to get back at her.

Joan needed to take back the power in this situation. First, she needed to stop investing in his relationship with their daughters because whether or not he saw them was out of her control. Whether their relationship with their father was ever meaningful or satisfying for the children likewise was not in her control. Fully accepting this reality was a struggle for Joan but she finally was able to.

Furthermore, Joan needed to name her ex-husband's behaviors

which gave her the greatest problems. In response to all inquiries about her personal life, Joan learned to answer, "That's none of your business." She learned to neither explain nor justify her actions, nor how she conducted her life.

Then came the matter of visitation. The next time he took the children, Joan told him to have them back before their bedtime or else take a motel room and return them in the morning, for she would not be home. When he failed to return them by 8:30 p.m., Joan put a note on the door, locked it and went to a friend's house for the evening. Her ex-husband was forced to spend the night in a motel with the children and returned them the next morning. From that point on, he brought them back on time, or even earlier, and he behaved in an increasingly responsible fashion now that there were real consequences for his behavior.

He even began to see more of his children since Joan was no longer invested in his doing so. She laid it out to him: "Whether you see them or not, or have anything with them, is up to you from now on. I'm out of it." Now he could no longer hurt Joan by ignoring the children.

The next situation Joan learned to handle differently involved pressure from relatives wanting a reconciliation. Joan needed to see her varied choices for taking back the power. The basic message she needed to learn to give was that reconciliation was no longer a topic of conversation. She could respond with something like, "One of the things that happens when you get to be an adult is that you can make your own mistakes." This would sidestep the confrontation. Or she could respond with, "Even if remaining divorced is wrong, it's still my way and I guess I'm stuck with it." Following either response, she would then need to change the topic of conversation in order to *behave* the message as well. If unwelcome comments persisted, Joan could then say, "Hey, this is not a topic for conversation. If there's nothing else for us to talk about, I guess I'll go for a walk." Again she had to actually behave the message when necessary. She could also choose to confront the matter more directly and say, "Look, I don't tell you how to live your life. Kindly don't tell *me*; it's none of your business." Then she could remove herself from the situation if that did not stop it: "Since you feel you have a perfect right to lecture me on what's good for me, I have a perfect right not to be around it." Joan was now armed with choices for how to respond differently to unwelcome intrusions into her privacy. Instead of trying to justify herself, and feeling resentful, Joan felt a new sense of power in relation to all her relatives.

Joan's depression lifted. She felt freer, brighter and had a renewed sense of hope. She found tangible ways for taking back her rightful half of the power in those situations which previously had left her feeling powerless, hopeless, and depressed. Joan learned new tools for living her own life more effectively and for becoming self-preservative.

Relationship Characteristics

There are several identifiable characteristics which emerge in the course of relating to other people. The first characteristic is the degree to which relationships are *genuine* and *honest*. The quality of genuineness refers to how much of ourselves we allow the other to actually see and experience directly in the relationship. When more of ourselves is emotionally present, we are being genuine. Likewise, honesty in a relationship includes honesty with ourselves as well as with the other. Honesty in a relationship means being honest about our feelings regarding the other's behavior. We must know both our own preferences regarding honesty and genuineness and how genuine and honest the other person can be.

Dependability is a second characteristic in which relationships vary widely. Dependability refers to willingly treating a relationship as a responsibility. Some individuals are quite dependable while others are not. One example of dependability is the extent to which an individual actually behaves in accordance with what he or she has said. Certain people blithely make promises which somehow never materialize. The matter of handling time is an especially curious instance. When some individuals say they will be somewhere at ten o'clock they mean ten o'clock while for others, it can mean anywhere between nine o'clock and twelve o'clock. As a rule, whenever there is a discrepancy between what people say and how they behave, it is wiser to listen to the behavior. That is always the honest message.

Honesty, genuineness, and dependability are vital characteristics of a relationship. We fare better in relationships when we consciously decide how we prefer our significant relationships regarding each one of these. Next we must consciously and objectively observe the other person involved in order to know that individual's capacity and preference for honesty, genuineness, and dependability. Only then are we able to strike a match between our own expectations and the reality of the other person.

A third characteristic to be considered when establishing relationships is *commitment*. Any relationship can involve essential elements of commitment. Even friendships can be lifetime commitments willingly entered into. Commitment in a relationship stretches well beyond the domain of love relationships by reflecting one's personal values regarding how one will behave in any relationship.

There is a fundamental trade-off in all of our relationships that is inherent to the question of commitment. In any relationship, commitment implies relinquishing a measure of personal freedom in exchange for gaining a measure of security. That loss of freedom can involve as simple a matter as now having to consider another's feelings and needs along with our own. The point of the matter is that commitment is on the wane in contemporary society; not everyone is either interested in a committed relationship or able to sustain one.

Noncommitment or a preference for unattached relationships involves a different choice. Here personal freedom is maximized at the expense of security. The time when the quest for freedom is naturally at its peak is immediately following separation from the family and before grappling with such essential commitments as career, life style, and marriage. Yet many individuals continue to remain uncommitted in their human relationships precisely in order to preserve their freedom at all costs.

Whether or not we are conscious of it, each one of us is making a choice regarding freedom vs. security in our relationships with other people. One young man has been struggling for some time precisely with this issue. He has tried to have both his freedom and the security which flows from human commitment. So many individuals similarly attempt to do so without realizing that can never work. Each choice in life is a package. Each choice brings us certain positive returns while at the same time costing us others. That is reality.

A type of relationship which is neither consistently committed nor consistently unattached, is the "In-and-Out" pattern. The "inner-outer" behaves precisely as the label suggests; such an individual moves in-and-out of relationship with others. An inner-outer can neither be depended upon nor predictable: now you see him or her, now you don't. There may be fine intimate times but these can not be counted on; following them, the inner-outer disappears for awhile, possibly a long while. These unpredictable disappearances can produce powerlessness and shame in the other person. Then quite suddenly, the inner-outer reappears as if there had been no absence. All one can do with such an individual is not expect the occasional intimate times to recur in any predictable or consistent fashion. It can be foolhardy to expect an inner-outer to be there when we *need* something.

Forming New Relationships

Let us examine closely useful principles for establishing new relationships. To begin with, we ought to pick someone we like who likes us. Too often we fail to consider consciously just how we feel about another. And we forget to listen for the essential cues which tell us how the other actually feels about us.

Once we have come across someone who interests us, we can let the other know clearly about our interest in having a relationship. We are taught in this culture to hide our real feelings or intentions and instead attempt to second-guess one another. If we all had graduated from a school for mind-reading this approach might succeed, but we must content ourselves with a more direct approach to establishing emotional ties. It works better early in a relationship to take a small risk and clearly say something like, "It'd be neat to get to know one another," or, "We could share some things," or even, "You're someone I like and would like to know better." Then we need to observe how the other responds to our invitation.

Imagine for a moment saying something like this to another person. Many times we quake in dread of their reaction, anticipating shame or embarrassment. It is essential that we be able to make such direct invitations to a relationship without any investment in how the other person will react. Our inner sense of worth or adequacy must not hang on the outcome. That alone allows us to risk freely because then there can be no injury to our self-esteem.

We must also be able to make such relationship starts without their having to work out. The other person may not be interested, may not have the energy for another relationship or simply may not want to. Whatever happens must not reflect upon our inner feelings about ourselves. It is precisely when our worth or adequacy is on the line that potential relationships become much too important and, hence, fraught with the danger of injury to self-esteem. That is when we are indeed afraid to risk. If we initiate a relationship offer and the other person is either not interested, cautious, or ambivalent, we must accept that fact without feeling rejected. Remember, no one can reject us unless we have first agreed to feel rejected. There is always that vital corridor of choice between life events and the meaning we attach to them. The only way this more direct relationship approach can work is if we simultaneously practice keeping our inner sense of worth or adequacy separate from whatever happens.

Relationships require practice over time. We would not expect to learn any other set of skills on the first few attempts, whether it be riding a bicycle, driving a car, or managing a restaurant. Each of these activities involves learning the necessary skills which, in turn, requires practice. It is no different with relationships except, here, the skills are interpersonal in nature. We must give ourselves "learning time," the time to make mistakes as we go about learning something new. And we must expect to practice if we are to become proficient at the craft of relating. Hence, let us risk and make our inevitable mistakes, but let us also take something useful from each one.

This philosophy of starting relationships is akin to fishing. We can cast often and widely on the sea of life, never knowing when or which of our relationship casts will be taken up by another. We must have no investment in the eventual outcome of any particular cast. Some do nothing for a long time. Others begin yet eventually fizzle or go nowhere. Then every once in awhile we get pleasantly surprised.

Once we have cast our relationship offer, we ought to take our time and wait to see how the other responds. Relationships fare better if we stay fully conscious and deliberately proceed slowly. Truly satisfying relationships evolve only over time.

It is much easier and more natural getting to know someone new around a shared task or activity. The relationship evolves in its own time and we come to know one another in an easy sort of way. No one feels on stage either. The activity or task itself provides a focus around which we learn about one another in a more realistic fashion. We get to see how the other responds to or handles various situations.

The more usual practice is the American dating institution in which two relative strangers come together for an extended period of time with the expectation: now we will be intimate. It is often an abysmal failure. It is unrealistic to expect strangers to be comfortable with one another, let alone intimate, in such an unstructured setting where the expectations of closeness run rampant. There is nothing more likely to kill the potential for closeness than *expecting* it. Hence, getting to know another person around an activity or task, such as a work or community project, hobby, or other interest, allows for a more natural, easy approach to establishing relationships. Then when those awkward silences occur, at least we can talk about the task or activity itself. Whenever getting to know someone new, it is useful to limit the time spent together until that easy comfort with one another develops.

We must also remember to keep our half of the power. This is accomplished, as already discussed, partly by not investing in whether the relationship actually works out and not attaching our inner feelings of worth or adequacy to how it fares. It is also accomplished through maintaining a position of equal power. Whenever we meet someone new we are faced with a choice. On the one hand, we can focus our attention on just how well or badly we are coming off. Worrying over how the other person is feeling about us is an inner stance which leaves us feeling relatively powerless in relation to the other. On the other hand, we can focus our attention directly on the other person, for example, on consciously observing that particular individual. When our attention is focused on objectively observing just what kind of person he or she is, this particular inner stance keeps us in a position of equal power.

In objectively observing the other person, we make a realistic and honest appraisal of that particular individual. Here we must step outside of our wishes, hopes, and fantasies about the other and see that person as objectively as possible. We must see the other as a package of strengths and weaknesses, as each person inevitably is. Let us review this process. Consider whether that person is capable of being genuine and honest, of sharing the power, of commitment, and of vulnerability. Consciously assess that person's basic values in living. Observe how this person handles his or her relationships. Remember to consult your own inner feeling reactions as well as the other's words and actions in order to know, for example, whether the other is genuinely warm or only capable of surface friendliness masking hostility underneath. Consider also whether the person is capable of relating emotionally, in the sense of being fully present in the *now,* or only cognitively, intellectually, without much real affective connection. Finally, observe whether the person is dependable: does behavior match the words?

The point of all this is not to avoid risks but to *risk consciously.* We are resilient; hurt or suffering will not diminish us. We need not fear pain. Let us learn from it and know something for tomorrow.

The foregoing characteristics must be known about others if our relationships are to strike a sound, realistic match between our own individual needs and expectations and the reality of particular people. No one is capable of meeting all of our needs. No one can be everything we desire. Each of our relationships will also be unique and different from all others. For example, we can be vulnerable with certain individuals, have other relationships for companionship, and still others for play. And of course, there are also many levels of vulnerability; it is not an all-or-nothing affair. There are degrees of vulnerability just as there are degrees of caring.

Not everyone is either interested in or capable of the same depth of relating. If we free ourselves from necessarily expecting to have the same quality or depth of relating with everyone, and if we consciously observe others to see what is realistically possible with each particular individual, then we are less likely to be disappointed and our relationships will fare much better.

The process of conscious objective observation of others is a skill requiring practice. Observing a person must be engaged in consistently over time in order to assess the reality of that individual. We must expect to consciously observe any given individual in a variety of situations over time in order to be able to decide what kind of person we are dealing with. Part of this process of objective observation involves "testing" the person in order to see if and how well we can trust that individual, or how honest we can be. We accomplish this by sending up "trial balloons" in order to see how well they fly. We can disclose something about ourselves, say, our feelings, reactions, or values, and then observe how the other reacts. If our trial balloon flies, then we can try another. But if it does not fly, meaning the other reacts badly, then it is wiser to wait before sending up another. Our trial balloon method is a way of sharing small vulnerabilities, a way of becoming progressively more open and honest about ourselves while, at the same time, being vulnerable wisely. It is a more conscious way to take the risks we need to take if we are to continue growing in our capacity for caring.

Now, in sending up these trial balloons, these disclosures of self, we are wiser not to expose a raw nerve too early in a new relationship. First we ought to disclose only those aspects of ourselves which are already *resolved;* that is, no current conflicts or raw nerves. Then, if our balloon happens not to fly, we are not hurt.

The approach to interpersonal relationships unfolding here is a very conscious one involving a number of skills which must be worked for actively. Relationships often do not come easily or naturally but indeed require learning.

Finally, having several relationships going, especially in the early stages, enables us to spread the investment and thereby maintain a position of power. If we have only one relationship, that single one becomes much too important; everything may hang on its outcome. Instead, if we have two or three going, what happens in any one of those relationships suddenly counts much less. We actually experience more choice that way and the more choices we have, the greater our sense of power.

Relationships are not inherently competitive. We are capable of caring about many individuals in different ways without having that detract from any one of those relationships. There is not some finite amount of love to go around which must be hoarded. We need to care, and care deeply, about others as well as be cared about. We must learn to navigate the world wisely, with power and caring, with power and vulnerability.

Staying Defended

Being vulnerable wisely requires us to know when and how to remain *defended* interpersonally. Having defenses with which to protect ourselves is both natural and useful: defenses arise because they have survival value. What is essential to living competently is developing conscious choice over our defenses so that we can choose either to engage our defenses or else to release them. When we are being open and vulnerable with another, we are releasing our defenses. However, we encounter many situations in which we need to keep our defenses consciously and actively engaged.

We need to first name our defenses accurately in order to have the choice over using them. For example, most introverts stay defended by withdrawing inside. Such internal withdrawal can manifest in keeping quiet when in certain interpersonal situations. Other individuals may behave just the opposite in tending to talk more as a means of defending the self. Anger can be employed as a defense to protect the self against shame. In order to know our defenses and then name them, we must work with ourselves consciously over time. Again, the principal tool is *consulting self.*

The times when it is wiser to stay defended by choice involve situations that are either hostile or competitive. In either case, allowing oneself to become vulnerable is precarious if not dangerous. While relationships are not in themselves inherently competitive, a competitive environment will make them so. Hence, it is usually safer and wiser to stay defended when navigating competitive environments. It is equally preferable to stay defended in new relationships.

Let us now translate this concept, staying defended, into action. Staying defended means not being vulnerable. Staying defended involves building a flexible, conscious shield about our innermost self. Staying defended also means remaining centered, fully conscious, and alert. It means not automatically taking inside and believing the messages communicated by others. Anything which hits our shield bounces off rather than coming inside and disquieting the self. That is precisely what staying defended means.

When we are defended in a particular interpersonal situation, we are fully conscious and alert. All defenses are engaged by choice. Staying defended also translates into the following: not looking for anything, expecting anything, or needing anything from that situation, person, or encounter. We are wiser not to look for approval, respect, valuing, caring, or emotional support from any individual until we have decided three things: first, that he or she actually has these to give; second, that he or she clearly wants to give these to us; and third, that there are no hidden price tags. Some individuals are apt to kick us after giving something emotionally while others expect to be "paid back."

Vulnerability

Now we come to the heart and soul of our relationships, *vulnerability.* To be vulnerable is to open the very self inside of us to another person *in safety;* vulnerability is openness without shame.

To be vulnerable is to share our most tender feelings and needs with another person. Whenever we experience and acknowledge our deepest needs—for relationship, for touching and holding, for identification and belonging or for separateness, to nurture another, or for affirmation and valuing—and do so openly in relationship with another individual, we are allowing ourselves to become vulnerable. Whenever we need from another or care about someone, we are vulnerable and inevitably relinquish a measure of power.

To need is to be vulnerable. To care is to be vulnerable. This is the heart of humanness.

Whenever someone becomes important to us, we have become vulnerable. We begin to allow another to matter deeply to us. We begin to treasure that other along with ourselves. In vulnerability we allow that person to enter our experiential world inside. We allow our most precious feelings and needs to be openly seen by the other without fear of censure. It is that experience of shared openness in safety which is the essence of human vulnerability.

Vulnerability is an opening of the self without shame, without feeling exposed or diminished. To be vulnerable is to experience openness *in union* with another, for it must be reciprocal to be real. The sharing of a vulnerability must be met by the other's like sharing of a vulnerability. That is what completes the experience and makes it safe, secure.

Consider a young boy who came home in tears, crying in response to some disappointment with a peer. He felt utterly free to cry openly with his parents in the safety of their home. They both comforted his pain and assisted him in understanding how to cope differently with the source of his distress. When he was done, and received his last hug, he looked up at them in certain trust through tear-clouded eyes, feeling safe in his vulnerability. Then he wiped his eyes and asked, "Are all my tears gone?" He returned to the outer world where staying defended is the wiser course.

As a basic rule it is wiser not to become vulnerable with someone unless that person has made it clear he or she also wants to be vulnerable with us. Then, it is also preferable not to expose a raw nerve too early in a new relationship. It is better to first send up a trial balloon, as mentioned earlier, and see how well it flies.

In moving a relationship along toward a more genuine, honest, and vulnerable level, one of the things we can do early on is share our feelings about the person. It is preferable to do this before strong feelings have actually built up. If the other person also values that kind of honest human sharing, we are encouraged to continue. This is a way of testing the waters to see how genuine and honest we can be with one another. The key, as always, is proceeding slowly and consciously observing the other's reactions over time.

When we are vulnerable with another person, we share the power. Some individuals, however, either lose respect or else pull back following the sharing of a vulnerability. The trial balloon method is most useful in discovering the other's characteristic response to vulnerability. What is most essential is learning to pick wisely those with whom we become vulnerable.

Security Relationships

Earlier, we explored building security within ourselves. We also build security through a network of *security relationships* with those key individuals who matter most in our lives. These are special people we depend on for our core emotional needs. We ought not look to everyone, or just anyone, for valuing, caring, or respect. The grouping of primary needs considered earlier can be thought of as security needs. We build a network of security relationships and look to these individuals for our most essential human needs. By having at least one, and preferably several of these security relationships, we actively establish security in the world.

These individuals will never be perfect; at times they will disappoint or fail us. That is to be expected in even the best of human relationships. But these individuals with whom we establish security ties are at least capable of honestly owning their own mistakes or failings. Vulnerability is mutual and power is shared. The relationship is genuine, honest, and mutually desired. Each is capable of commitment to the relationship and willingly treats the relationship as a responsibility, something to be nurtured, even treasured.

These special individuals may be parents, relatives, or friends. They can be peers or mentors. When it is a peer relationship, a relationship among equals, each can offer support to the other. If it is a mentor with whom we have established a security relationship, we will likely turn to this esteemed individual whenever we need to feel affirmed, to feel that vital sense of valuing as a unique self, or to feel recognized and openly admired. At other times we may look to such a person for essential guidance in living life; we may also turn to this special teacher in order to experience identification and belonging. We never wholly outgrow our need for having someone who is older and wiser to serve as a guide in life, a teacher in living.

It is both natural and good to need emotionally from others, but we must pick wisely. Either our early learning or the culture teaches us to feel inadequate or shameful about having needs, but to need is to be human.

Intimacy:
Fluctuating Closeness and Distance

In any on-going relationship, periods of intimacy or closeness will naturally fluctuate with periods of emotional distance. To expect to feel close or loving all the time is never realistic in any relationship, let alone an enduring partnership. It is more realistic expecting periods of distance to alternate with periods of closeness. Periods of distance may or may not be brief. The key is accepting distance as natural; it is neither a crime nor a rejection.

John and Susan, married seven years, had been worrying about their relationship for some time, thinking that love had gone out of it. Their prior closeness was seemingly absent. Once they realized that distance was as natural as closeness they were no longer quite so worried. In fact, taking the pressure off allowed intimacy to return of itself. They also learned to rekindle it through special ways of nurturing their relatonship. Setting aside an evening for a late candle-light dinner alone or taking a weekend vacation together were tangible ways to renew caring.

Too often individuals feel rejected and shamed when the other partner does not feel especially close or intimate. It is necessary to be clear with one another about each partner's needs and to respect the other's needs however out of synch they may be. We can care about one another's feelings without feeling responsible for them. And we can care about each other's needs without necessarily feeling responsible for meeting them. Though we do not feel close or loving all the time, we must have faith that these feelings will return.

Power in Relationships

The craft of relating involves learning how to integrate power with vulnerability. Vulnerability is essential but wise only when the power is shared. Allowing ourselves to care and be cared about are the essence of humanness, but caring with power is its quintessence. Hence, we need to develop and maintain *equal power* in our relationships whenever possible. Whenever we need something or expect something from another individual, whether peer or parent, we are surrendering a measure of power to that other person. It is also especially useful to keep alert for situations or relationships in which we feel powerless and/or trapped. Powerlessness is a seedbed for shame in whatever circumstance, context, or relationship it arises.

Let us consider several relationship examples involving the uses and abuses of power. The first one involves a young woman, Carolyn, in a graduate program in the sciences. While the context may seem at first remote, the issue and its handling are instructive for us all and also transferable to many other situations we are apt to encounter. Carolyn ran into conflict with a fellow student with whom she had to share a laboratory. Carolyn was a responsible person; when she used supplies or equipment she returned everything to its place, clean and in good repair. Her lab partner never washed the equipment he used; Carolyn would often end up washing his as well as her own. This produced powerlessness, followed by rage. She attempted to confront him about the matter, but his promises to do better never translated into behavior. There was nothing she could do to *make* him do his share of the work. She then brainstormed the matter and identified various choices available to her for taking back the power. Carolyn finally decided to keep her own private supply of lab equipment locked in a cupboard. Then one day when the general supply had run out, she quietly observed her partner loudly complaining that he had to wash everything before he could work. There was no one to bail him out and Carolyn no longer felt powerless or enraged. She had taken back the power.

So many times when individuals attempt to work or live together, marked power imbalances surface to disturb the relationship flow. Consider the situation when individuals share the same living space. When one roommate does not carry his or her share of the load, resentment is the usual result. One of the individuals might not wash his share of the dishes but instead leave them for the others. If such a pattern persists beyond just an occasional occurrence, this will likely create ill feeling. In order to offset such an eventuality, discussion or confrontation can be one attempt at solution. More often, action

speaks louder than words. Letting the other's dishes actually accumulate in a separate corner will likely produce quicker results than
any amount of diplomacy. By not doing the other's share of the work,
resentment is avoided, power is maintained, and natural consequences will take effect to correct the other's behavior.

Words do not always avail us in human affairs; they do not always
stimulate a real change in behavior. Changing our own behavior in a
situation will often require a change on the part of others. The
situation itself has been changed through our behaving differently in
it.

Consider this next situation as a further illustration. Steven and
Andrea, each in the process of divorce and with children of their
own, were beginning a love relationship. Early on, he made it rather
clear that marriage or commitment of that sort was entirely out of the
picture for him. Once was quite enough, thank you. She, on the other
hand, continued to hope for eventual remarriage. Clearly their expectations were mismatched.

Other troubles more directly affected their day-to-day contact.
Andrea was the kind of person who fully intended to carry through
with whatever she said she would do, while Steven behaved differently. On numerous occasions, Steven would tell Andrea he would
either come over later that evening or would be calling and then
never do so. She would drop her plans and wait for him, fully
expecting him to call or arrive. This would often leave her feeling
disappointed or hurt, taken for granted, powerless, and enraged.
When she asked him what had happened, he would either say that he
had become engrossed in some activity or else had forgotten. He
promised it would not happen again, but it did.

His behavior in their relationship continued to raise her expectations and then leave her disappointed. Andrea finally attempted
direct confrontation by expressing how she felt in response to his
behavior. Steven felt bad about causing her grief, was penitent and
said he could certainly understand how it must feel to her. Yet the
pattern continued.

Since several direct confrontations had produced little actual results, the way to take back the power, in this case, was for Andrea to
change her expectations of the relationship to match the reality of
Steven. She needed to see that their long-range expectations regarding commitment were entirely mismatched. About that at least he

had been honest from the outset. The pattern which caused her so much grief was part of the package that was Steven; whether it ever changed was not in her control.

Andrea had to learn not to count on, literally not to expect, Steven behaving the way he said he would. On any given occasion, if he promised to call or come over, Andrea had to expect that he might not show up. Likewise, she could no longer drop whatever plans she had made on the chance of his arriving or calling. There were times when she had readjusted prior plans for the weekend because he said he would be calling to set something up with her and then he never called. By no longer putting aside what she had planned, Andrea learned how to keep her own rightful half of the power in that relationship.

Their relationship continued over some months until Andrea fully accepted that what they shared was genuine and intimate when it occurred, but she could not safely expect such experiences with any degree of regularity or predictability. If she could be content with whatever they shared together at any point in time, with no expectations beyond that, then they could indeed sustain a relationship. To do so meant not looking for anything more than a somewhat unpredictable pattern of occasional intimacy or companionship. Clearly, he was either not interested in, or not capable of, commitment to a relationship in the way she needed. Andrea realized over time that she could certainly keep her expectations in check and in line with reality. But what she could then safely have with Steven was not much of a relationship from her view. It would not meet her basic needs nor was it the kind of relationship she particularly valued. In order for her to invest emotionally in a relationship, the other person also had to behave in a sufficiently committed fashion through all those day-to-day occurrences which are the stuff relationships are made of.

Becoming Partners:
Sharing the Power

Power comes sharply into focus in any partnership or marriage in a number of important ways. The first of these is dividing areas of responsibility. Consider the following: who will provide the financial support for the family, assuming there is one? Who will be primarily responsible for raising the children or will that task be shared somehow and, if so, how? And who will handle the basic tasks of living and managing the home or will that, too, be shared jointly? There are no correct ways of resolving such matters that will work for all couples. Yet these are matters of enormous importance whenever two individuals attempt to live together under the same roof. Certain of these issues come into especial focus only when children enter the picture. Prior to that juncture matters may seemingly handle themselves well enough even if no conscious attention is paid to them. However, a conscious attitude toward dividing areas of responsibility in any partnership will serve to keep the power in balance.

Consider Tom and Terry, who are married and have two children. Before they had children and while each worked full-time, no serious problems surfaced in their relationship. Yet a few years later, constant arguing ensued about who was to do what regarding the children and home. One of the things they did to identify the sources of their difficulties was to write out their expectations of themselves and each other as concretely as possible. When they exchanged lists, they were surprised by the result; their fundamental expectations of their relationship were out of synch. Tom expected himself to be bread-winner and supporter of the family while his wife was to raise the children and manage the home. Terry's expectations were that the two of them would have separate careers and share equally in both raising the children and managing the home. She had been attempting to change Tom in order to make him fit her expectations while he wanted her to behave in accordance with his expectations of a marriage.

Individuals usually bring two sets of expectations into a marriage. People often fail to make all of them conscious to see how well they match. Any two people will have different needs, likes, and preferences regarding almost everything. Couples need to work out through negotiation what is mutually satisfying for them. Each must care about the needs and feelings of the other. Too often we presume upon others, forgetting they are separate, with rights and feelings of their own. Making requests involving service or time highlights an important arena where power can become imbalanced, resulting in one partner feeling used and taken advantage of. For example, a man who has his own business and expects his wife to do the bookkeeping *because they are married,* even though she works full-time raising their child and managing the home, will likely create powerlessness and resentment. We do not have the right to expect service on our behalf without the other having free choice.

How money is dispensed or handled and financial decisions made are also direct reflections of power within a relationship. Certain questions must be considered consciously in working out suitable financial arrangements: Is all money earned to be kept joint, or is it to remain separate? If it is all joint, who has control over spending it and over money earned separately? If all financial decisions must be joint ones, how are different spending priorities and different spending styles to be reconciled?

Let us proceed by way of example. Mike and Alice, each working full-time, are in their second marriage. In his late fifties and a full professor in the sciences, Mike has never liked his career. He is anxious to leave it and pursue some new, more satisfying interests, but to do so would require his wife supporting the two of them. Alice was willing to do this through the transition. About a month after leaving his position at the university, Mike began feeling powerless and his self-esteem was markedly diminished. He no longer felt productive or knew who he was. He entire sense of identity had been thrown into crisis: he had nothing he could call his own.

In our society, identity, self-respect, and self-esteem are essentially grounded in productive work, in feeling ourselves contributing. Mike had freely given that up and thrown himself into a state of temporary identity confusion. What was more, he now had to ask Alice for any money to spend. Mike felt acutely powerless.

The reality of his utter financial dependence left Mike feeling like a beggar whenever he wanted to buy something however personal or necessary. That feeling was intolerable. The solution worked out was a monthly spending allowance for Mike so that he could have a portion of the resources to call his own. That resolved part of his crisis and made the rest more manageable, especially after he realized the natural consequences of the choice he had made.

Power needs to be shared in a relationship for two people to feel themselves equal partners. Insofar as such matters as dividing responsibilities and handling money are considered consciously, or perhaps even agreed upon before individuals actually marry or live together, they will have a means for knowing how well matched their respective expectations are. Furthermore, they will discover how well they are able to negotiate as equals, to resolve essential differences respectfully and satisfactorily, and to build a relationship in which each is sensitive to the needs and feelings of the other.

The essential thing is not only those perplexing issues which must be given attention in a relationship. It is not even the varied guidelines themselves which, however vital, matter most in what we have been considering. What is of deepest consequence is an approach to relationships which is uniquely conscious in its intent, its attitude, and its moment-to-moment expression in living.

Redefining Relationships With Parents:
Attaining Equal Power

The transition from adolescence to adulthood has been blurred in contemporary society. With so many individuals continuing to college and requiring financial support, adolescence itself has become prolonged. There can be no claim of adulthood until one begins actually behaving as an adult. Fully taking the reins of one's own life is the hallmark of adulthood. And we lack for accepted and meaningful rites of passage. Is it at age eighteen that we become adult because we can vote or are we adult when we graduate from college? Does marriage make us adult or do we need to enter a trade, career, or profession? We are unclear and ambivalent as a society about the business of coming of age. We vote in the age of majority and a few years later we may decide to change it. In some of our states, eighteen year-olds are old enough to vote and bear arms, but not to drink alcohol. Such cultural contradictions confuse the transition to adulthood even further. The extensive financial support provided by parents to their adult children does likewise.

Consider Peter, a graduate student in professional school who continued to take considerable amounts of financial support from his parents. Periodically, he was subjected to lectures on how he was spending too much money and was an awful person. On other occasions, the lectures took the form of admonitions about how long he was taking to get through school. Comments about his academic performance came at still other times. Between these recurring lectures, Peter continually felt guilty about spending their money and he felt enraged at his parents because he felt guilty. Usually, we are apt to resent whomever we perceive as "causing" us to feel guilty. Peter felt additionally obligated to his parents for all the money they provided him. This left him feeling indebted.

When family celebrations occurred, holidays were imminent, or school was in recess, Peter never felt altogether free to visit or not as he chose. Because he had taken their money, he felt obligated to "pay back" somehow, if only in visits home. At twenty-nine, Peter neither felt like an adult nor behaved as one. Quite the contrary, he felt not only guilty and resentful towards his parents but powerless as well. This was the harvest he reaped from the unwitting choice he made to remain financially dependent on his parents well into adulthood. In this way, he and his parents colluded in prolonging Peter's adolescence indefinitely. This situation is a widespread cultural phenomenon, especially so in a technological society where young people are enjoined to continue in the lengthy cultural apprenticeship we call higher education. The emotional price paid is a dear one.

In choosing to take his parents' money, Peter quite naturally felt a measure of indebtedness to them. Whenever we take significant amounts of money from someone, we are likely to feel similarly obligated. That is the natural consequence of the choice. Along with feeling obligated, we relinquish a measure of personal freedom and in so doing, surrender a vital measure of power. If he had borrowed money from a bank, all of the terms would have been spelled out well in advance along with the interest charge and date upon which the loan would be paid back. In taking money from his parents, Peter was paying "emotional interest" which included his feelings of guilt, resentment, and obligation. This meant that they could reasonably *expect* visits home because they were supporting him. Peter never felt like an equal adult, able to freely say yes or no, because he was taking their money.

His parents naturally felt a right to lecture him on how he spent their money or on how he progressed in school, which might be viewed as the return on their investment. Had he either fully earned his own way or borrowed the money to do so, he could easily dismiss all of their lectures on behalf of his self-improvement. Since he had chosen to be supported, he could not in good conscience do so. In taking their money, he inadvertently laid himself open to being told how to live his own life. One cannot expect to be treated as an adult until one requires it of others, parents included, through finally behaving as an adult by fully taking the reins of one's own life.

What was to be done? After realizing the predicament he had

gotten himself into, the next step was identifying his choices for extricating himself from it. Peter had a source of income through work in the university. He needed to see whether he could manage without taking money from his parents. After he got over the initial shock of this rather sobering thought, he realized he could indeed survive. It would be a bare-bones, survival-level existence, but he would not go hungry and he would have a roof over his head, though it would certainly be a far cry from his accustomed standard of living. Now he had a real reference point. His basic choice was this: how much of his creature comforts was he willing to forego in exchange for diminishing the emotional interest he had been paying? Since he had to suffer in any event, at least he now had a choice and could realistically choose between different kinds of "suffering."

Peter had yet another choice. Should he decide to continue taking a measure of financial support from his parents, he could actually change its ground rules from a "free ride" to a loan. He could set up the arrangement precisely as he would if he borrowed money from a financial institution. In this way, Peter would not feel quite so obligated to his parents or indebted to them. He would no longer feel guilty and would derive a greater measure of self-respect as well. The arrangement would now become one between equal adults and Peter would, at last, be moving toward a position of equal power in relation to his parents.

If adulthood has any meaning, it must lie in attaining a position of equal power in relation to other adults and especially one's biological parents. Adulthood without equal power is a sham.

Each emerging adult ought to be accorded a position of equal power in relation to parents. This translates into calling the shots for our half of the relationship and setting limits on how we will allow others to treat us. Furthermore, it is essential for children who have grown into adults to consciously decide what they feel they owe their parents. Even when there is much joy in what we share with our parents, the profound and difficult question each of us must ponder is this: what do we feel we *owe* our parents given what they gave us? Relationships between children and the parents who raised them carry elements of obligation. It is imperative to distinguish what *we* feel we owe our parents from what *they* feel we owe them. Knowing precisely what we owe in such concrete terms as phone calls, visits, and participation in family events frees us to know what we might actually *want* to share or give. We must also know the emotional costs of any continued interaction. These guidelines enable us to decide what kind of relationship we want to have with our parents as equal adults.

This is heresy in our culture. There is no model or support for approaching relationships with one's biological parents in such a conscious fashion. Even though honoring one's parents has been an accepted ethical principle, is it not ultimately up to each individual to decide how to do so? This departure from custom and tradition is required of us if we are to live consciously and stay centered in a position of power in our lives. We must adjust this cultural dictum to match the honest reality of individual situations. Far too often, relationships with parents remain clouded, infantile, or burdened by guilty obligation.

It is our individual conscience which must guide us, to which we must answer for our conduct in the end. It is a task not lightly undertaken and we must be able to live well with whatever decision we make.

Karen was living with a man, to her parents' displeasure, and was going home to tell them of her intention to marry him, fully expecting the coming storm. All she really desired was her parents' respect and affirmation of her as an adult. Karen realized she was powerless in expecting this, for she could not make them give it.

She went home completely defended and quietly told them of her plans. When her mother hotly objected, refused to pay for the wedding and doubted whether she would even attend, Karen simply and firmly responded: "Well, mother, that's your choice. We'd like you there if you want to come. If not, it can't be helped." Her parents were stunned; they had nothing to say.

When participating in family celebrations is expected of us, many individuals feel resentful. Those of us who do, need to experience a choice over whether and how we will participate in future family celebrations. Only when we know which of these we owe our presence at are we ever free to say yes or no to the remainder. There are times when we in fact will be a disappointment to our parents or other relatives. This is to be expected in life and cannot be helped if we are to live our lives guided from within.

Relationships between parents and children must evolve into relationships between equal adults. That is the natural end toward which parenting itself must aim if we are to raise autonomous individuals. "There is no more trying, more stormy task in life than parenting. Bringing a new human being into this world, then nurturing this emerging self into an adult who is capable of living his or her own life competently, with dignity and affirmation, is a challenge which knows no bounds. Parents invest eighteen years of themselves in care-taking which, if it is done right, culminates in letting go. To give so fully of oneself to this unfolding new person only to one day open that family door, watch with respect mixed with sadness as this newly becoming adult steps forth alone, and then set aside the robes of parenthood, requires a painful greatness."[2]

Translating Theory Into Action:
Creating Tools

The following tools enable us to become more conscious of our particular needs and expectations and to observe others objectively. Learning to match expectations with reality is the goal.

TOOL #1: OBSERVING RELATIONSHIP SCENES
What am I looking for in this relationship?
What am I needing from this person?
What are my expectations from this human relationship?

TOOL #2: HOW POWERLESS VS. EQUALLY POWERFUL DO I FEEL
IN THE RELATIONSHIP?
Identify situations in the relationship which represent both of these.
To what extent do we share the power in the relationship?

TOOL #3: TO WHAT DEGREE DO I EXPERIENCE SHAME IN THE
RELATIONSHIP?
Identify instances of shame.
When and how often do I feel shame?
Can I express these feelings to the other?

TOOL #4: HOW GENUINE AND HONEST CAN WE BE WITH EACH
OTHER?
Can we honestly admit our wrongs and our own failings?
Can we be vulnerable with each other and feel safe?

Can we confront one another with our feelings and feel both listened to and heard?
Can I confront the other and know the other will be honest both with self and with me?

TOOL #5: COMMITMENT AND THE TRADE-OFF BETWEEN SECURITY AND FREEDOM
How much commitment do I need in a relationship?
How committed does each of us feel to the relationship?
Are my needs and feelings cared about as well as the other person's?
Do we each willingly treat the relationship as a responsibility?
How important is personal freedom to each of us vs. security?

TOOL #6: OBJECTIVELY OBSERVING THE OTHER PERSON
Make a realistic and honest appraisal of that person by listing their " + 's" and " − 's."
See the total package that the other person is, with strengths as well as weaknesses.
Try to see the other person objectively, apart from your fantasies, wishes, and hopes.
Is the other person capable of being genuine and honest, of sharing the power, of commitment, of vulnerability, etc.?
What are that person's basic values? Dreams?
How does this person handle relationships?
Is this person genuinely warm or only superficially friendly but hostile underneath?
Does this person relate emotionally or only cognitively?
Do this person's behavior and words match?

TOOL #7: MATCHING EXPECTATIONS
When two people are involved in or considering marriage, a partnership, or some form of committed relationship, it is useful for them to make conscious their expectations and then see how well they match. The following are some aspects to consider:

 1. Commitment to the Relationship
 2. Sharing the Power/Negotiating Decisions
 3. Dividing Areas of Responsibility
 4. Managing the Home
 5. Handling Money and Financial Decisions
 6. Having Separate Interests and Careers
 7. Having Separate, Outside Relationships
 8. Time Spent Together vs. Time Spent Separately
 9. Relationships with Parents and In-laws
10. Interest in Having Children
11. Child-rearing Practices
12. Sex
13. Future Dreams

The Tools in Action:
Experiences From the Course

Alice spoke first about her life and relationships: "Matching expectations with reality is very difficult for me. I always look for the good in people and situations and feel guilty about being critical. Therefore I'm not selective and I get burned over and over. Even after getting burned, I'm incredibly quick to forgive and likely to get burned again. I somehow have the idea that it's wrong to advance myself, to make something of myself, to be selective and choose what is good for myself. The point is this: I never learned to be selective, to make choices, to observe people and situations. Hence, I don't know how to see the realities and I don't know what I have the right to expect. I don't know when I have the right and opportunity for something better or when I need to simply accept the imperfection in a situation."

Ken discovered: "It was interesting to evaluate a relationship and, after writing what seemed to be a book, I wasn't finished. It made me see how passive I allow myself to be and I recognized my feelings of powerlessness—which I don't combat but, rather, accept." Sally talked about her sister: "I have withdrawn a lot from the relationship after many years of staying with it. I finally saw that she wasn't willing or able to give me things I always kept hoping for. I can get them from other people. I don't feel obligated to love her just because she's my sister. This is only the beginning of a change, but it's a pretty auspicious beginning after 40 years."

The theme of power was a recurring one. Barbara told us: "I made the most progress in the area of power in relationships. Two important ones stand out. With my rich sorority perfectionist friend, I carved out some ground rules. I quit being competitive and I started a friendship. With my Dad, I learned to say no." Randy spoke about his experiences: "I've been trying the tools of observing people and sending up trial balloons. Too often in the past, I've waited for the other person to take the initiative." Steve followed: "Learning to observe people has helped me not assume that everyone is polite, respectful, responsible, and fair. I am now a closer observer of people." Howard reported the following changes: "I find myself being more aware of my own expectations from relationships and aware of what others might be expecting from me. Recently, I've become more assertive in setting limits in situations where I felt the individual was having expectations that I couldn't meet. I've also become cognizant of power and it's really helped me take back the power with my parents. I'm also conscious of power in my relationships with women. At times I had become so attached to someone that I gave her a lot of power and made myself too vulnerable."

All of these individuals learned useful tools for navigating the human world with greater competence. One must practice building relationships in order to become proficient at this craft.

Caring With Power

All of the preceding considerations must be blended with basic human caring if we are to have mutually satisfying relationships. It is good to care and it need cost us little, for caring truly nourishes us as well as others. We can care in stages, without necessarily becoming too vulnerable all at once. The goal is not to hoard caring in the service of the self, but rather to be willing to take small risks now that we know how, to reach out often and meaningfully touch others, and to be vulnerable wisely. Living consciously is the soundest course for learning how to care with power.

CHAPTER 5

Caring, Attachment, and Commitment in Crisis

In a society grown as complex as ours, it becomes especially urgent to maintain inner security and self-esteem, which are essential to competent living. We live in an age of cultural crisis and there is nothing like powerlessness and uncertainty to shake our confidence. We are uncertain about the environment and energy, about the health of our economy, about the future of marriage and the family, about our children, values and political leaders, all of which undermine our confidence and threaten our belief in the future. Navigating this Age of Uncertainty requires skill and confidence. All about us, men and women renounce compassion and caring. The profound dilemma we face in navigating the world is learning how to care deeply yet be vulnerable wisely. That is the challenge of the age in which we live.

Attachment and Commitment in Jeopardy

Our society is fostering growing tendencies toward noncommitment. There are several factors contributing to this result. Until recently, the cultural expectation was that everyone would marry. Such a commitment was valued above all and consequently, many married who did not want to. Now the pendulum has swung the other way, bringing with it greater cultural acceptance for alternate lifestyles including partnerships without marriage as well as remaining single. The enhanced freedom we now enjoy to choose our own path is certainly useful, even vital. However, we are seemingly purchasing that freedom at the expense of commitment.

Another source of the contemporary reluctance to care with commitment is the serious reality of marital failure. Young people no

134

longer believe that relationships can endure. Either they have experienced divorce directly or instead witnessed marital breakups within their peer group. Our media contribute to their dilemma through graphically advertising the failure of marriage, and observational learning is as potent a teacher as direct experience. Many young people have said, "I've never seen marriage work so why bother trying." The failure rate for marriage cautions many against embarking upon similar ventures. Even children in grade school have come home and asked their parents, "When are you and daddy getting divorced?" as though it were inevitable. Divorce is not merely a reality: it is a cultural expectation. In such a climate, commitment is becoming a vanishing value.

Our cultural context is continuing to be shaped by societal mobility which directly encourages us to treat relationships as temporary. Accelerating societal mobility is altering fundamental expectations concerning permanence. We have created a society in which individuals are on the move: we expect to move repeatedly after even a few years. People who are transitory are less likely to invest deeply in relationships or establish enduring emotional ties. This is essentially self-protective. We feel safest to invest ourselves completely in relationship with another when a sense of permanence surrounds our mutual caring. However, when the other person expects to be leaving, we inevitably experience a natural human tendency to diminish our emotional involvement. We are least likely to make commitments in a transitory environment. Pulling back is a way of protecting ourselves against any eventual loss.

Our cultural context of accelerating mobility is altering our capacity for meaningful and enduring human attachment. We are learning to insulate ourselves against recurring losses by restricting the depth of intimacy and its continuity over time. Individuals need to experience a viable personal future, thrive only on believing that they have a future to live for. Relationships require no less. Our relationships depend upon predictability, stability, and continuity for maturation; they are nurtured by that vital sense of having a future, thereby thriving on commitment. It is our capacity for commitment which is eroding; having a succession of temporary relationships is the new and prevalent pattern of contemporary society.

The foregoing factors contribute to a spreading avoidance of commitment, broadly conceived. Relationships with other people are being treated increasingly as transitory. Instant intimacy is our new cultural expectation.

William Kilpatrick has described the contemporary dilemma of commitment in telling words:

> "It is precisely this that contemporary man finds so difficult to do. He does not want to choose. He does not want to give up any of the possibilities. Indeed, he wants to taste all possibilities without ever having to choose among them. He looks about him at the many attractive identities from which to choose and fears that any exercise of choice will limit him to something less than his appetite for variety demands. The media show him more possibilities than he ever dreamed of, with new ones appearing daily on the horizon. Television makes him feel that he is missing out on these possibilities, so does the press when it devotes an article to the latest life-style, and the polls of his neighbors' sex practices only add to his feeling of being left out and left behind. So he goes dashing about hoping to partake of all these possibilities, choosing none of them. He wishes to postpone commitment until a more convenient time—that is to say, indefinitely."[1]

The challenge of the decades ahead is precisely whether we will reclaim the value of commitment. To do so requires an understanding of its impact. Identity is rooted both in future scenes of purpose and in choices. The purposes we hold dear, which give life its meaning or direction, reflect our life goals and give us a future to live for. These goals continue to shape our sense of identity. Likewise, through the array of fundamental choices we make, we define our essential self. By our choices we become known to ourselves and to others. Identity is rooted in choice; to refuse choice and commitment is to throw identity itself into crisis.

Caring vs. Competitiveness

While competition, achievement, and success have been the banners of our time, having genuine and honest relationships cannot easily coexist with excessive competitiveness in human affairs. Is it safe for competitors to be genuine, honest or vulnerable with one another? Of course not. Competitors cannot risk letting down their guard; they must always maintain a decided edge over others. This is true in the *family* when children are encouraged to compete with each other for tangible rewards or parental acclaim. Encouraging children who live together in one family to always compete to see who is the better, smarter, or more popular will of necessity discourage their being real, honest, or vulnerable with one another.

While a certain amount of natural competition is inevitable, a family ought to be a place where being human matters more than seeking one's advantage or being best. We can live the values of caring and compassion, we can model honesty with ourselves and one another, and we can ensure vulnerability in safety. A home is a place where one can feel safe to be truly who one is, where one does not have to guard oneself.

Encouraging competition will have parallel consequences in *school settings*. Consider the case of graduate programs designed to train professionals. Insofar as those students are stimulated to compete with each other for grades, supervisors, placements or internships, and especially for financial support, it becomes imperative to keep either abreast or ahead of the pack. Outdoing all other competitors for the limited resources available becomes the widely encouraged mode of survival. Many may argue that this is precisely the way to select the best; however, the price paid is a loss of humanity.

Some graduate school programs employ a different concept of education: only as many graduate students are accepted as can be supported. Hence, competition is not additionally stimulated by the nature of the program itself. A certain amount of natural competition will occur anyway, but students will not perceive one another as active competitors. In such a climate, compassion and cohesiveness are enabled to flourish; students can afford a little warmth with one another. Graduate students in more competitively designed programs complain about the lack of fellowship among their peers. They wonder why close relationships with their fellows are for the most part lacking. Their own hunger for simple human caring must be satisfied elsewhere.

The *work setting* is a third arena where competition reigns. Wherever competitiveness is the predominant ethic other coworkers will find themselves striving to outdistance one another. Even when we are not so inclined, a competitive atmosphere will alter our attitudes and behavior. We begin to compare ourselves to one another; we begin to measure who is the more productive, successful, or esteemed. We begin to compete for recognition. Our relationships inevitably suffer because competitors cannot afford to care too deeply about one another.

If we seek to foster and preserve our essential humanity, then competition must be held in check. If we instead encourage competition, then we inevitably discourage honesty, caring, and vulnerability. The choice is as clear as that and all choices have their consequences. In choosing for competition are we not ultimately creating a society of indifference? And does not the potential for violence become greater in a climate of indifference?

Caring For Our Children

Selma Fraiberg argues that experiencing either a *succession* of care-givers or *indifferent* care-givers particularly in the earliest years may lead a child to defend against the loss by not attaching to other people later in life.[2] Certainly there are countless instances when the use of outside care-givers is unavoidable. Such is the case with women who choose to work for personal or career reasons, with single-parent families, with families in which one parent is disabled or ill, and in situations of financial necessity. Children understand necessity and will adapt to it as required. And mothers who must work or have chosen to do so for personal reasons may be fortunate indeed in locating quite satisfactory substitute child care.

We must, however, remember to consider the psychological impact that either a succession of full-time care-givers or indifferent care-givers will have, whether through day-care centers or babysitters in the home, upon especially young children regarding their future capacity for human attachment and commitment. Certainly further study and research are needed. Fraiberg raises important questions regarding the wholesale use of a succession of care-givers, particularly when these are indifferent ones, as though such a practice had no serious impact. Children learn through the actions of parents and other adults who play a vital role in their world. What children require for the optimal development of their capacity for love, trust, and self-worth are stability, continuity, and predictability in their relationships with care-givers, whether biological or surrogate. Caring about children with commitment will also teach children how to care with commitment.

Fraiberg carefully considers the potential impact upon children of a succession of care-givers, especially indifferent ones:

> ". . . If a mother of an infant or preschool child can freely choose to work or not to work, she can ask herself the questions. If she chooses to

work full time for personal reasons, or career reasons, she can examine her options in terms of her child's needs and her own needs and make her decision on the basis of the best information available to her and the real choices she has in substitute care.

"If she *must* work for financial reasons, her options for substitute care are poor and there are almost no good solutions open to her—at least so far—which serve the needs of her child.

"I am worried about millions of children who are being served by Child Care Industries Incorporated. I worry about babies and small children who are delivered like packages to neighbors, to strangers, to storage houses like Merry Mites. In the years when a baby and his parents make their first enduring human partnerships, when love, trust, joy, and self-valuation emerge through the nurturing love of human partners, millions of small children in our land may be learning values for survival in our baby banks. They may learn the rude justice of the communal playpen. They may learn that the world outside of the home is an indifferent world, or even a hostile world. Or they may learn that all adults are interchangeable, that love is capricious, that human attachment is a perilous investment, and that love should be hoarded for the self in the service of survival.[3]

The point here is by no means that women should not work, but rather that there are almost no good alternatives at present for quality child care which also serve the emotional needs of children. A fine surrogate mother may be found, but what happens when this second mother later departs? Continuity can be a serious problem and too many losses may well teach a child that it is not safe to commit.

Child care centers present an analogous problem with regard to continuity and consistency of relationship between child and the adult or adults serving as surrogate parent. There is additional evidence, as Fraiberg points out, that while young, preschool age children will profit from a half-day of day care, they will cease to benefit educationally and may even begin to deteriorate somewhat emotionally toward the end of a long, full day's separation from home and the principal parent. Furthermore, the nature of the emotional involvement between care-giver and child, whether occurring at a day care center or at home with a babysitter, is paramount. This is in addition to the problem of continuity.

The psychological impact, especially upon preschool age children, of experiencing a succession of care-givers must be seriously weighed along with that of experiencing indifferent care-givers. What we need is a national priority, to echo Selma Fraiberg, for developing useful and sound alternative child care programs which satisfy the psychological needs of children.

If attachments are made to adults who become significant and these attachments must later be broken when those adults depart, and then new attachments must form to yet new adults, followed perhaps by another series of ruptures and losses, and so on, is there a point at which a young child will stop attaching in order to protect itself against these recurring losses? Furthermore, if children are left in the principal care of indifferent care-givers, is there an analogous point at which they will cease attaching in order to, in Fraiberg's words, hoard love for the self in the service of survival? If there is indeed such a point in either case, are we not raising a generation of individuals whose capacity for attachment and commitment is impaired? What does that bode for the future of our society?

Caring and Vulnerability:
Culture in Transition

If we are ever to create a truly caring society, then we need people who know how to care and care deeply. We need people who care about people, social conditions, our environment, and our future. We must value caring and teach people how to care just as we teach them how to live with a sense of power in their lives.[4] Caring is the soul of human vulnerability and the soil from which we spring. The vulnerability inherent in caring is as much an expression of our humanity as power is. They complete one another.

Whenever we allow ourselves to care deeply about another, we are inevitably susceptible to shame, disappointment, or loss. Caring and pain are interwoven. Our capacity to feel hurt is, even further, a measure of our capacity to care. Pain is the touchstone of caring; to deepen our capacity for caring is to deepen our capacity for suffering.

Vulnerability has grown out of fashion; it is not especially useful in a culture with disposable relationships. If we are to be mobile, being vulnerable is a liability. As we insulate ourselves from pain, loss and the inevitable suffering inherent in enduring human attachments, what price are we paying for our cultural choice? What kind of individuals are we raising in a society where commitment is being replaced by a succession of temporary relationships? What will be this generation's capacity for caring, attachment, and commitment?

Will our young people be made more flexible for a rapidly changing world, or rendered more insulated and indifferent, less capable of compassion or empathy for the less advantaged or suffering, less capable of caring beyond the convenience of the present moment? Will they have a self with which to keep faith, a self to commit to anything, or will honesty and integrity have become inconvenient in tomorrow's world? What kind of people will evolve in a society where vulnerability, caring, and commitment have become inconvenient?

If caring diminishes, if there are fewer enduring attachments, we will reap a harvest of indifference and alienation. What will restrain the natural aggression of human beings? What will curb violence? Will anyone even care?

Humankind is at a turning point in its evolution. Culture is in transition. And the fate of nature's human experiment hangs in the balance of the choice which remains ours alone to make.

In a society which values achievement and success through competition, we are repeatedly stimulated to seek our advantage over others, contributing to fear and hatred. But we can no longer live by advantage alone. Our world has grown too close and we will, hopefully, rise to the challenge handed us by our own, self-created crises. We must *cooperate* with one another, and with nature, if we are to survive at all. Otherwise, alienation and powerlessness will only accelerate and further contribute to the diminishing of enduring human bonds.

As the distance between people and power grows greater, cracks will inevitably widen in our social matrix. To echo the words of Jacob Bronowski, we must not perish by that distance. And that distance can only be closed if the knowledge and skills of psychological health are made available so that all individuals can live more wisely, with dignity and affirmation, with power and caring.

Notes

Chapter 1

[1] Bronowski, J. *The Ascent of Man.* Boston: Little, Brown and Co., 1973, p. 435.

[2] Frankl, V.E. *Man's Search for Meaning: An Introduction to Logotherapy.* New York: Pocket Books, 1963, pp. 104–105.

[3] Kilpatrick, W. *Identity and Intimacy.* New York: Dell, 1975, p. 43.

[4] We are indebted to Dinny Kell for the concept of the happiness and adequacy tools.

Chapter 2

[1] Kaufman, G. *Shame: The Power of Caring.* Second Edition. Cambridge: Schenkman, 1985, pp. 112–115.

[2] We are indebted to Dr. Jean Houston for the concept of this tool.

[3] We are indebted to Tom Burdenski for this suggestion.

Chapter 3

[1] The principal sources have been Bill Kell, Dinny Kell, Silvan Tomkins, Erik Erikson, Harry Stack Sullivan, Viktor Frankl, Carl Jung and W. Ronald D. Fairbairn. For example, Silvan Tomkins made the critical distinction between the affect system and drive system while Bill Kell, Harry S. Sullivan, and W.R.D. Fairbairn began the exploration of the need system. Viktor Frankl laid the equally essential groundwork for what is herein named the purpose system.

[2] For a detailed discussion of shame and its impact on identity, see Kaufman, G. *Shame: The Power of Caring.* Second Edition. Cambridge: Schenkman, 1985.

[3] Frankl, V.E. *Man's Search for Meaning: An Introduction to Logotherapy.* New York: Pocket Books, 1963, p. 120.

[4] Simonton, O.C., Matthews-Simonton, S. and Creighton, J. *Getting Well Again.* Los Angeles: J.P. Tarcher, 1978.

[5] Tomkins, S.S. *Affect, Imagery, Consciousness,* Vol. 1 and 2. New York: Springer, 1963.

[6] A fine book detailing the fusion of shame and disgust with the hunger drive is Eda LeShan's *Winning the Losing Battle: Why I Will Never be Fat Again.* New York: Thomas Crowell, 1979.

[7] Frankl, V.E. *Man's Search for Meaning: An Introduction to Logotherapy.* New York: Pocket Books, 1963, pp. 116–117.

[8] Kaufman, G. *Shame: The Power of Caring.* Second Edition. Cambridge: Schenkman Publishing Co., 1985, pp. 109–112.

[9] For an excellent guide to meditation see Lawrence LeShan's *How to Meditate: A Guide to Self-Discovery.* Boston: Little, Brown and Co., 1974.

[10] We are indebted to G.I. Gurdjieff and P.D. Ouspensky for this conception: Nicoll, M. *Psychological Commentaries on the Teaching of Gurdjieff and Ouspensky.* London: Watkins, 1975.
Ouspensky, P.D. *The Fourth Way.* New York: Vintage Books, 1971.

[11] We are indebted to Dinny Kell for the concept of this tool.

[12] LeShan, pp. 82–84.

Chapter 4

[1] For a more in-depth discussion of the impact of shame on adolescence, see Kaufman, G. *Shame: The Power of Caring.* Second Edition, Cambridge: Schenkman Publishing Co., 1985.

[2] Kaufman, G. *Shame: The Power of Caring.* Second Edition Cambridge: Schenkman, 1985, pp. 59–60.

Chapter 5

[1] Kilpatrick, W. *Identity and Intimacy.* New York: Dell Publishing Co., 1975, p. 43.

[2] Fraiberg, S. *Every Child's Birthright: In Defense of Mothering.* New York: Basic Books, 1977.

[3] Fraiberg, pp. 110–111.

[4] See Kobak, D. "Edu-caring: Teaching Children to Care by Developing the 'CQ' or Caring Quality in Children." *Adolescence,* 1977, 12, 97–102.

Bibliography

Adler, A. *The Practice and Theory of Individual Psychology.* Patterson, N.J.: Littlefield, Adams and Co., 1959.

———. "Individual Psychology" In *Psychologies of 1930,* edited by C. Muchison. Worcester, Mass: Clark University Press (1930): 395–405.

———. "The Psychology of Power." *Journal of Individual Psychology,* 22 (1966): 166–172.

Ansbacher, H.L. and Rowena R., eds. *The Individual-Psychology of Alfred Adler.* New York: Basic Books, 1956.

Bronowski, J. *The Face of Violence: An Essay with a Play.* Cleveland: World, 1967.

———. *The Identity of Man.* Garden City: Natural History Press, 1971.

———. *The Ascent of Man.* Boston: Little, Brown and Co., 1973.

Buss, A.H. and Plomin, R. *A Temperment Theory of Personality Development.* New York: John Wiley, 1975.

Combs, A. W. "Humanistic Education: Too Tender for a Tough World." *Phi Delta Kappan,* February 1981, 446–449.

Dreikurs, R. and Stoltz, V. *Children: The Challenge.* New York: Hawthorn Books, 1964.

Elkind D. *A Sympathetic Understanding of the Child Six to Sixteen.* Boston: Allyn and Bacon, 1971.

Erikson, E.H. *Childhood and Society.* New York: Norton, 1963.

———. *Identity: Youth and Crisis.* New York: Norton, 1968.

———. *Toys and Reasons: Stages in the Ritualization of Experience.* New York: Norton, 1977.

———. *Identity and the Life Cycle.* New York: Norton, 1980.

Fraiberg, S. *Every Child's Birthright: In Defense of Mothering.* New York: Basic Books, 1977.

Frankl, V.E. *Man's Search for Meaning: An Introduction to Logotherapy.* New York: Pocket Books, 1963.

———. *The Will to Meaning: Foundations and Applications of Logotherapy.* New York: World, 1969.

———. *Psychotherapy and Existentialism,* New York: Simon and Schuster, 1968.

Gendlin, E.T. *Focusing.* New York: Bantam, 1981.

Goleman, D. "Meditation and Consciousness: An Asian Approach to Mental Health." *American Journal of Psychotherapy.* 30 (1976): 41–54.

Gould, R.L. *Transformations: Growth and Change In Adult Life.* New York: Simon and Schuster, 1970.

Jennings, E.E. *The Executive in Crisis.* New York: McGraw-Hill, 1965.

Kaufman, G. *Shame: The Power of Caring,* Second Edition. Cambridge, Mass., Schenkman Books, 1985.

Kaufman, G. and Raphael, L. "Relating to the Self: Changing Inner Dialogue." *Psychological Reports,* 54, (1984): 239–250.

Kell, B.L. and Burow, J.M. *Developmental Counseling and Therapy.* Boston: Houghton Mifflin, 1970.

Kierkegaard, S. *A Kierkegaard Anthology.* Edited by Robert Bretall. Princeton: Princeton University Press, 1946.

Kilpatrick, W. *Identity and Intimacy.* New York: Dell Pub. Co., 1975.

Kobak, D. "Edu-Caring: Teaching Children to Care by Developing the 'CQ' or Caring Quality in Children." *Adolescence, 12* (1977): 97–102.

———. "Teaching Children to Care." *Children Today,* 8 (1979): 1–4.

———. Curriculum for Caring. *Instructor,* 89 (1979): 53–57.

Lane, H.A. *On Educating Human Beings.* Chicago: Follett Pub. Co., 1964.

Lane, H.A. and Beauchamp, M. *Human Relations in Teaching.* New York: Prentice Hall, 1955.

LeShan, E. *Winning the Losing Battle: Why I Will Never Be Fat Again.* New York: Thomas Crowell, 1979.

LeShan, L. *How To Meditate: A Guide to Self-Discovery.* Boston: Little, Brown and Co., 1974.

Levinson, D.J., Darrow, C.N., Klein, E.B., Levinson M.H., and McKee, B. *The Seasons of a Man's Life.* New York: Alfred Knopf, 1978.

May, R. *Power and Innocence.* New York: W.W. Norton, 1972.

Mayeroff, M. *On Caring.* New York: Harper and Row, 1971.

McClelland, D.C. *Power: The Inner Experience.* New York: Irvington Publishers, 1975.

Montagu, A. *Touching: The Human Significance of the Skin.* New York: Harper and Row, 1972.

Nicoll, M. *Psychological Commentaries on the Teaching of Gurdjieff and Ouspensky.* London: Watkins, 1975.

Ouspensky, P.D. *The Fourth Way.* New York: Vintage Books, 1971.

Pelletier, K. *Mind as Healer, Mind as Slayer: A Holistic Approach to Preventing Stress Disorders.* New York: Dell Publishing Co., 1977.

Postman, N. "TV's 'Disastrous' Impact on Children." *U.S. News and World Report,* January 19, 1981: 43–45.

Raphael, L. and Kaufman, G. "How to Talk to Yourself—And How Not To." *Successful Woman,* 6 (1984): 6–7.

Seligman, M.E.P. *Helplessness.* San Francisco: W.H. Freeman and Co., 1975.

Shapiro, K.J. and Alexander, I.E. *The Experience of Introversion: An Integration of Phenomenological, Empirical, and Jungian Approaches.* Durham: Duke University Press, 1975.

Sheehy, G. *Passages: Predictable Crises of Adult Life.* New York: Dutton and Co., 1974.

Simonton, O.C., Matthews-Simonton, S., and Creighton, J. *Getting Well Again.* Los Angeles: J.P. Tarcher, 1978.

Singer, J.L. *Imagery and Daydream Methods in Psychotherapy and Behavior Modification.* New York: Academic Press, 1974.

———. "The Scientific Basis of Psychotherapeutic Practice: A Question of Values and Ethics." *Psychotherapy: Theory, Research, and Practice.* 17 (1980): 372–383.

Singer, J.L. and Pope, K.S. *The Power of Human Imagination.* New York: Plenum Press, 1978.

Sullivan, H.S. *The Interpersonal Theory of Psychiatry.* New York: W.W. Norton, 1953.

Thomas, A. and Chess, S. *Temperment and Development.* New York: Brunner/Mazel, 1977.

Toffler, A. *Future Shock.* New York: Bantam Books, 1970.

———. *The Third Wave.* New York: Bantam Books, 1981.

Tomkins, S.S. *Affect, Imagery, Consciousness, Vol 1 and 2.* New York: Springer, 1963.

Wheelis, A. *The Quest for Identity.* New York: W.W. Norton, 1958.

White, R.W. "Motivation Reconsidered: The Concept of Competence." *Psychological Review,* 66 (1959): 297–333.

Winter, D.G. *The Power Motive.* New York: The Free Press: 1973.

Index

Growth, personal
dynamics of, 4–5, 22
and observation, 5
Guilt, 41, 42, 102, 126

Happiness
expectations for, 23, 32–33
personal responsibility for, 6, 33
tools for collecting and storing,
23, 24, 25–26, 34
Happiness List, tool of, 23, 24, 25–
26, 34
Health, physical, and state of mind,
63
Health, psychological, x, 29, 44, 57,
68, 83, 84
and education, x, xviii, 2, 141
key dimensions and principles of,
xviii, 30–34, 43
Homophobia, definition of, 45
Humor, and detachment, 74
Hunger drive, and affect, 64

Identification, with significant
others, 36, 59–60
Identity, 30–51, 136
and choice, 10, 11, 136
development of, xv, 36, 67
and personal creations, 21
and productive work, 125
separate, 61, 97
and shame, xiii, xiv, xv, xvii
Imagery, 71, 75, 83–86
and tool for letting go, 86, 87, 93
Inner child, 45–47, 52
and tool of reparenting imagery,
4, 47–48, 50–52
Inner relationship. See
Relationship, inner
Inner voices, 36
observation of, 37–38
replacement of, 38–39
tools for changing, 47, 48–49
Integration. See Self, integration of
Internalization, 21, 36
Interpersonal need system, xv

Intimacy
in a relationship, 9–10, 100, 104,
120
and shame, xiii, xvi, xvii, 99
Introverts, 44, 104, 117

Journal writing, xvii

Kierkegaard, Søren, 11
Kilpatrick, William, 136

Language
and affect system, 56–57
development of, 53
and differentiated owning, 54
and living consciously, 12, 53
and power, 57
of the self, 12, 54–68, 72
Living consciously, 1, 5, 11–12, 53–
94, 104, 129, 133
and choice, 22
and the conscious self, 53–54, 82,
94
key dimensions of, 11–12, 82–83
and language, 12, 53
tools for, 86–89
See also Conscious self;
Detachment; Imagery;
Naming; Owning,
differentiated; Self-observation

Manipulation, of others, 102
Marriage. *See* Partnership
Matching Expectations, tool for,
131.
See also Expectations, tools for
matching reality and
Meditation, as tool for detachment,
79, 86–87, 93
Mistakes, attitudes toward, 34–35
Montagu, Ashley, 59
Motivation, 62, 66
Motivational systems, xv, 15, 55
See also Affect system; Drive
system; Need system; Purpose
system

BIOGRAPHICAL SKETCH

GERSHEN KAUFMAN was educated at Columbia University and received his Ph.D. in clinical psychology from the University of Rochester. Currently he is a professor in the Counseling Center at Michigan State University. He is the author of *Shame: The Power of Caring*, (Schenkman Books, 1985), *The Psychology of Shame: Theory and Treatment of Shame-Based Syndromes* (Springer Publishing Co., 1989), and *Journey to the Magic Castle* (forthcoming 1992, Double M Press). He is the coauthor with Lev Raphael of *Stick Up For Yourself! Every Kid's Guide to Personal Power and Positive Self-Esteem* (Free Spirit Publishing, 1990).

LEV RAPHAEL was educated at Fordham University and received his MFA in Creative Writing from the University of Massachusetts at Amherst. He holds a Ph.D. in American Studies from Michigan State University where he has taught as an assistant professor of American Thought and Language. With Gershen Kaufman, he codeveloped and co-taught the program, "Psychological Health and Self-Esteem," on which *Dynamics of Power* and *Stick Up For Yourself!* are based. His fiction has appeared in *Redbook, Commentary, Men on Men 2* (New American Library, 1988), *Midstream, Christopher Street, Hadassah,* and *The James White Review.* He is author of *Dancing on Tisha B'Av* (St. Martin's Press, 1990) and *Edith Wharton's Prisoners of Shame* (St. Martin's Press, 1991).